You've Got a
What?
in your
Where?

**An Inside Account of life and work within an
NHS Accident and Emergency Department**

T.J. Edwards

Shield Crest

© Copyright 2013 T. J. Edwards

All rights reserved

ISBN: 978-1-907629-81-5

MMXIII

Published by
ShieldCrest,
Aylesbury, Buckinghamshire,
HP22 5RR   England
www.shieldcrest.co.uk

To my husband Gareth, and children Katie, Sarah and Dominic. Thank you for putting up with the many rants and complaints that I have so often brought home after a hard day's work at 'the sharp end'.

You make it all worthwhile.

The Author

TJ is forty something years old and a Registered General Nurse. She is married with three grown up children and lives in the South of England.

After several years working within the field of dentistry, she began her General nurse training in 1983 in Warwickshire and realising that, although she loved working with people, general nursing was a lot more appealing.

Newly married in 1988, she moved with her husband to a pretty holiday island on the coast to take up a post within a small cottage hospital there. Following the closure of that hospital, she moved to the Accident and Emergency Department within the General Hospital on the island, where she works as a senior staff nurse.

Preface

"You've Got a What in your Where?" is not authorised or endorsed by the National Health Service, it is merely a collection of events during my years within that fine institution.

Events have not necessarily been placed in strict chronological order, as literary licence has been needed at times.

All names of patients and staff have been changed in order to preserve confidentiality, anonymity and downright embarrassment. The name of the principal hospital and some place names have also been changed.

Many people working within the NHS, and particularly the Accident and Emergency Department will find that lots of the stories contained within this book are somewhat familiar – the settings may change, but human beings do not.

CONTENTS

≈ 1 ≈

In the Beginning

"I rather think you should be eating *that* in the staff room" – and so began Christmas Day 2008. Another Christmas day spent with my other 'family', my colleagues in the Accident and Emergency Department and the legion of human detritus that passed through on that particular day. I have given up counting just how many Christmases, birthdays and other important dates have been spent mopping up beds and people, filling out numerous pieces of paper and telling other people that "It's alright, that's what I'm here for." when I want to be anywhere other than "here".

I have been working in Accident and Emergency for over a dozen years, having moved on from working in the operating theatre. I had got a bit fed up with my patients being mainly asleep and uncommunicative and had been desperate for them to talk back. Moving into the Accident (A/E) Department meant that they communicated their needs, wants and likes to me - in spades! Most of the time that was greatly appreciated, as being able to give a patient effective pain relief when necessary and to make them comfortable just by helping them to change position is very satisfying and is, after all, why I went into nursing in the first place. Having personal observations made about my height (lower end of average), weight (slightly above higher end of average) and personal characteristics (quirky, but reasonably 'normal') are less appreciated, but go with the job.

I have wanted to go into nursing for as long as I could remember, possibly something inherited, as my mother was a nurse and, in fact, had met my father on the surgical ward that she was working on. He was a rather poorly patient that she had to 'special' (one to one nursing which is reserved for the most ill patients) and after recovering he asked her out. One thing led to another and in 1964 I came along.

I cannot recall ever wanting to be an air hostess or a hairdresser like the rest of my friends. I flirted briefly with the idea of owning a sweetie shop but that was based on pure greed (and a sweet tooth) and the idea didn't last long. I just presumed that I would be a nurse when I grew up and after passing the required O levels, duly began training in Warwick.

Our training was divided up in to specialities, some of which took place at outlying hospitals, and those of us who lived in nurses' accommodation were expected to move to where we were working. Our general medical and surgical nurse training took place in Warwick, but the three months of midwifery training was at the specialised maternity unit five miles away, and our geriatric and psychiatric training was at various cottage hospitals out in the Warwickshire countryside. The nurses' accommodation was very similar to University Halls accommodation: many single rooms off a long corridor in a large building presided over by a 'home warden' – and two sides of A4 paper worth of regulations, mostly covering who you could have in your room to visit (parents, same sex friends and colleagues) and who you couldn't (anyone of the opposite sex, unless it was a father, brother or other relative). Amazingly, many of us trainee nurses suddenly had 'brothers' appear out of the woodwork, whenever a male was spotted leaving our rooms by the Home Warden. Six o'clock was the cut off point for ANY man being in your room and each time that we moved to a new accommodation block at another hospital there was a scrabble for a ground floor room – particularly for those that overlooked the car park at the back! The occasional fire drill always produced amusement and panic as student nurses filed out through the front door, while out of the back of the building, men were seen to be climbing out of various windows along the length of the Home.

As student nurses, we spent a lot of our time doing repetitive tasks such as the taking of observations. The 'Obs' round consisted of recording the blood pressure, pulse, respiration and temperature of every patient on the ward, and could be quite time consuming. These days, various machines are used and when attached to the patient, can read the blood pressure, pulse and respiratory rate all at once, and a digital tympanic thermometer in the ear can check the temperature within five seconds. The result of this is that each patient can be checked within a few minutes, as opposed to the lengthy 'rounds' of the early 1980s. After a while, you got into the routine of checking all twenty odd patients on the ward sometimes four times a day – and my own routine was similar to many others'. At that time, we used glass mercury thermometers, which were placed under the patients tongue. The thermometer had to stay in place for at least three minutes, and the most effective way of ensuring that this happened, would be to go around each patient in turn placing a thermometer under his/her tongue, and then removing each as you went back round from bed to bed recording the rest of the patients' observations. Being charged with doing the round one morning, I started by placing thermometers under the tongues of the first six patients before I was approached by one of the trained nurses who asked if I would like some help. I accepted gratefully and, as I was about to place the seventh thermometer, the patient asked the trained nurse assisting me what the difference was between the thermometer I had in my hand, and the one in the mouth of the patient in the next bed.

"The thermometers with the white end are normal thermometers, and the blue-ended ones are for rectal use" she said.

I don't know who was more shocked – me, who hadn't realised that these pretty thermometers were any different, or the patient in the next bed who immediately spat the thermometer out of her mouth!

It is a well-known and traditional practice for student nurses to be the butt of practical jokes, no matter what ward or department they are working in. In fact, any junior or inexperienced staff member was fodder for the sort of wind-up that occurred regularly while I was training.

We had just been instructed on the importance of pressure area care in immobile patients on the orthopaedic ward when Sally, a fellow first year student, was asked by one of the staff nurses to "pop over to ward 6 for an air-ring". Ward 6 was a medical ward situated on the ground floor and had a pair of double doors that led out to a small garden area. Sally was directed to the double doors and told "it's out there". Confused, but eager to complete her errand, she went through the doors, which were then shut behind her. After a few moments, the doors reopened to show a couple of grinning nurses who said that she could come back in now that she had had her 'airing'. This sort of practical joke was repeated several times during my time in orthopaedics but I was lucky in not being a preferred victim.

A personal favourite of the trained nurses on one of the female medical wards was to put some heavily diluted orange juice in a urine pot and then show the students how to do a pregnancy test. When the test showed up as negative they would say "No, she's not pregnant, but I think she has diabetes." They would then sniff the pot before taking a large sip and stating "Yes, definitely diabetic!" If *that* didn't put students off medical nursing, then nothing would.

One of my last placements during training was in theatre recovery and I must admit to sending a very green first year student to 'wait over there' when she came into the unit for a 'long stand'. She had been sent by one of the senior nurses for a 'special' drip stand that was longer than the ones that they kept on her ward!

Three and bit years after starting my training, I somehow passed my final exams, became a fully-fledged RGN (Registered General Nurse) and was let loose on the general public at Warwick Hospital.

Moving On

Not too long after qualifying, I married and moved to a small island just off the coast to begin working at the Cottage Hospital there – a wonderful little hospital with just 12 medical beds and, upstairs, a small surgical unit dealing with minor surgery. I was only there for a couple of years before the hospital closed, as is the way with many cottage hospitals now, but my time there was both rewarding and fun. Being such a small hospital, the staff all worked as a tight knit team and we all got to know each other very well. There was one Sister in charge and the day to day running of the hospital was the responsibility of Sister Katherine.

The Nursing Officer made a visit maybe once a week and it was always down to one of the junior staff nurses to watch out for her car coming down the steep drive and send out the word "Hazel's coming!" Playing cards would be put away, beds straightened and patients put on their guard – those were the days that we nurses had time to sit and play cards and chat with our elderly patients between doing drug rounds, wound dressings and various other procedures. However, even though looking after the emotional welfare of our patients was just as important as the physical side, it was still frowned upon and all evidence was hidden during the weekly visits by The Boss.

The days spent at the cottage hospital were enjoyable and, as we were situated on the top of the cliff, the views from the work place were spectacular. It was here that I learned how to ride in the 'dumb waiter' by pressing the 'up' button from the outside of the lift and then pulling your arm in sharply before it became amputated as the lift rose upwards; that it was possible to slide down the large mahogany banister if wearing tights with your uniform dress (but never in stockings) and that if you stretched cling film tightly enough over the staff toilet and then put the seat down, you can't tell that it's there!

This was actually arranged as a 'surprise' for Sister one day, but before Katherine got to use the 'little girls room', the cry of "Hazel's here" resounded across the surgical floor as the Nursing Officer appeared unplanned and a lot earlier than her usual time. Her first stop was to the staff toilet, and most of us nurses hid in the sluice not sure whether to be horrified or delighted. A good fifteen minutes later, the front door was heard to open and close, and Hazel's little mini was seen hurtling up the driveway. Nothing was ever said about that incident, but when we eventually ventured out of the sluice we found that that the tiled floor in the staff toilet had been thoroughly cleaned and was nice and shiny!

≈ 3 ≈

Christmas Day

A few years and couple of nursing jobs later, it's Christmas day 2008 and *that* reprimand. Usually, Christmas Day in Accident and Emergency is a little more relaxed: after all, the patients want to be here even less than we do. All of the staff fill out a 'snack list' up on the staff room wall before Christmas, denoting what nibbles we will be bringing in to work, and then every free moment over the Christmas period is devoted to nipping down to the staff room for a quick bite to eat. This is a great novelty as it is not unheard of to work for six to eight plus hours without any time to grab food or a cuppa. Most nurses (and other A/E staff) manage to work with rock bottom blood sugar levels and six pint capacity bladders!

The offending item of food had been brought in that morning by Ellen. Her husband was a dab hand in the kitchen and had made some enormous fresh cream profiteroles for her to bring into work. Knowing that they would disappear in minutes, and having a load of paperwork to do, I decided to sneak an extra-large pastry into the department proper to eat while working. I thought I had done quite a good job of hiding it when Ian's voice came from behind me. Ian was the nurse in charge that day, and although great to work with, he was a stickler for the rules. Caught in the act there wasn't a lot I could do, other than take my forbidden treat into the staff room – while Ellen smirked from the other side of the desk, having just hurriedly swallowed the one that she had been eating at the same time. Some people are just born to get away with things! Needless to say Ellen didn't own up, and I hadn't the heart to 'dob her in'. After all, it was Christmas Day.

Aside from that transgression, the rest of the day continued no different to many other days, with a steady stream of minor accidents and various illnesses.

Eleven o'clock saw a young mother arrive with a piece of bloody tissue held around the tip of an index finger. A quick chat and the examination showed that she had nicked the top of her finger with the vegetable knife whilst cutting the carrots for Christmas dinner. It was a very superficial cut, needing just a single steri-strip to hold the edges together, but the patient was insistent that it needed stitches and asked for a 'second opinion' to check if stitches were possible. While trying to establish why someone might actually *prefer* to have stitches rather than non-invasive paper strips to treat a wound, her mobile phone rang. On the other end of the phone was her husband, demanding to know when she would be back as he, their three children, his brother and his parents were awaiting her return so that she could finish preparing the dinner – they were quite concerned that their meal would be late and he reminded her that she had also yet to prepare the desserts! Not once was any concern shown for her painful finger and, although the poor lady didn't have the stitches that she requested, she did leave the department with a bulky finger bandage, a sling, and written instructions to keep the offending digit clean, dry and rested!

As the day wore on, minor accidents and 'generally unwell' patients gave way to those that had overeaten and over indulged in alcoholic beverages. With the GP surgeries being closed, Accident and Emergency becomes a magnet for people who have deviated from their normal routine and 'don't feel right'. One such patient was Harold, a gentleman who had consumed a large quantity of malt whisky before lunchtime, and was convinced that the world was falling out of his bottom. After finding that his blood pressure, pulse and heart rhythm were perfectly normal, Harold was waiting patiently on a trolley in the department for the results of his blood tests. While waiting for a good couple of hours for the lab to get the blood tested and the results put on the computer, Harold explained that he had had stomach pains for over a week now, and they had actually got worse since he was given medication by his GP. He said that not only did the suppositories not work, but he now had bleeding from his back passage. Knowing that any rectal bleeding is potentially serious, I questioned him a bit further. I established that he had not been taking the suppositories orally as I first suspected (it certainly wouldn't be the first time that I had heard of a patient swallowing suppositories or pessaries and wondering why they are not working), and so was still none the wiser. Unfortunately, we were not particularly busy during the afternoon and I had time to stay with Harold while he regaled me with the history of his rectal bleeding. Nice. I asked him if he knew what the suppositories were called and to try and help jog his memory, I showed him the glycerine suppositories that we had in the department. "That's the buggers", he exclaimed when I took them out of the box to show him "and the corners are bloody sharp when you put them in!" It appeared that poor Harold had been inserting the suppositories with the hard plastic outer wrapper still on.

≈ 4 ≈

Confused?

Shifts in A/E were certainly never dull. Busy, annoying, frustrating and downright exhausting, but never dull. And colleagues can be just as entertaining as the patients. Amongst the staff, two of the nurses had epilepsy, two were insulin dependent diabetics, three had asthma and one was coping with a chronic back problem – her spine had a tendency to 'lock' resulting in temporary immobility. Despite the best attempts of whoever was setting the rota that week, quite often some of the patients were in better condition than the staff. If only they knew! It certainly wasn't unusual to be missing a member of staff, only to find that they were occupying a trolley in the next bed space – but it was all part of the variety of life within the department.

Katy, a junior staff nurse, had been struggling with her diabetes control for some time and when she couldn't be found during an evening shift, a subtle alert went out to find her and check she was ok. Not finding her in a cubicle, and establishing that all the single rooms were empty, one of the other staff nurses walked into the waiting room to call through the next patient. The waiting room contained only one patient – and a large yucca plant that Katy was patiently trying to get a triage history from! It appeared that her blood sugar levels had dropped too low and Katy was a tad confused. No matter how many times it was explained to her, she remained convinced that the yucca plant needed some analgesia and a course of antibiotics! It certainly wasn't the first or last time that one of us had taken Katy into the staff room and force fed her a Mars bar.

More often than not though, it was the patients who were confused and many is the time that I've asked basic questions of a patient to ascertain their mental state, only to realise that I don't actually know the day or date myself. Usually, the patient is elderly, but not always. Shaun was just 15 years old and part of the influx of rugby players that are regular visitors during the rugby season. Sporting seasons are well defined within the Accident and Emergency department and many Saturdays during the autumn and winter see the department full of muddy rugby boots and filthy kit. Shaun had clashed heads with another player during a scrum and knocked himself out for several minutes. A consequence of this injury was that the lad had a decent concussion and resulting confusion. Whilst awaiting a CT scan to determine that there was no permanent brain injury, Shaun asked me what he was doing on a trolley in hospital and how he had got there. I explained the sequence of events as best as I could and he seemed satisfied. Two minutes later, he asked me again where he was and why. I repeated the sequence of events and again, Shaun was happy. Two minutes later, he asked where he was, and why! Patience is a virtue and, patient though I am, I stayed with Shaun for just another five or six minutes before persuading another nurse to take over from me and see Shaun through his scan. By that time, I had repeated the events more times than I could count and was pondering on the merits of delegation. As I left Shaun in the capable care of Mandy, I heard him ask "How did I wind up on a bed, and where am I?"

≈ 5 ≈

Keep it Clean

Working in a high pressure A/E department can have its light moments, and at times this is at the unsuspecting patients' expense. A gentleman booking in at reception wearing a long wool coat and citing a 'personal problem' definitely piques the interest of most of the staff. James certainly did have a 'personal problem' and seeing how uncomfortable he was, I bypassed the triage room and took him straight into a side room for privacy. Removing his full length coat revealed a solid length of vacuum cleaner hose attached to his penis. Somehow, James had been "hoovering in the nude" when he "accidently dropped" the hose, which had managed to attach itself to his penis! Suction and the subsequent swelling of tissues had done the rest. Sometimes it is hard to maintain an impassive face and not say "yeah, and I was born yesterday".

Whilst taking a history in the side room, word of sorts had obviously got around the department and it was quite incredible the amount of staff who needed to pop in to "get something out of the cupboard" or to ask if I was holding the drug keys. Sometimes, you just need to see for yourself!

≈ 6 ≈

Education

Part of working in an environment and within an occupation that is constantly evolving is the requirement of frequent updating and education. This further education quite often takes the form of study days, either internally or at another hospital. Our departmental manager, soon to become a 'modern matron', decided to send a quartet of staff to a study day in London in order to learn a little more about suicide and sudden unexpected death, and dealing with the relatives in the immediate aftermath of such an event. Such a subject should not be a recipe for either humour or light heartedness, but then we were A/E staff – and odd at the best of times.

Travelling up to London were June, Cassie, Barry and myself, all nurses. Going anywhere with Barry was a bit hit and miss and rather like travelling with a hyperactive child. Barry is two years older than me, but has the mind, and lopsided humour, of a teenage boy. Travelling almost a hundred miles to London in a tin can on wheels, with a grown man who finds farting funny, can be a bit wearing, but that was just the start. Arriving at the study day venue, we discovered that the majority of the other attendees were social workers or police officers. Pleasant though they were, I felt that these professionals were on a slightly different wavelength. The day started with a senior social worker, who told a story of a bereaved family who were greatly helped by her providing them with a cottage pie in their hour of need! For some reason, this tickled all four of us and the day became dubbed the "Cottage Pie Study Day".

Of the four of us, Cassie had been awake all night with a sick child and kept falling asleep – not too obvious in itself, but as she was sleeping sitting in a chair, snoring was inevitable. June had a back problem and could not get comfortable in her seat, and spent most of her time shifting about noisily, much to the annoyance of those seated around us. That left Barry, with his intermittent offensive flatulence, and myself, and we were both still giggling like schoolchildren about the mention of cottage pie being a bereaved family's salvation. It was rather like breaking loud wind in church – suddenly everything became very funny and despite the disapproval of the other 'students', we just couldn't behave like grown-ups! The day concluded at around 4pm and not a single one of us could recall having learned anything (except for the merits of cottage pie). This was not something that we would be telling our manager, as the department had sent us on this course to learn and then to return to the department and impart our knowledge to the rest of the staff.

Travelling back along the motorway in June's car we realised that our ferry to the island left in ten minutes – and we were fifteen minutes away. Barry decided that come what may we were getting that ferry and, getting June to pull over on the hard shoulder, he got out of the car, walked round to the driver's side and, ordering June to 'budge over', got into the driver's seat. He put his foot to the floor — and, breaking every speed limit in the book, we caught the ferry! Hair-raising, yes, but at least we got home on time.

≈ 7 ≈

Food for Thought

Accident and Emergency nursing, by its very character, tends to attract male nurses, and we had quite a healthy proportion of male to female care staff across all grades.

Our men ranged from the quiet and softly spoken John, an Emergency Nurse Practitioner in his late fifties, to Kevin, a young junior staff nurse who dashed around like a whirling dervish and was more effeminate than some of the female staff. We also had our share of 'foreign imports', amongst them Joe, an Australian national who – by his own admission – "didn't much understand kids". Although some of the staff were specially trained to treat children, we all looked after both children and adults and Joe was no exception. A small boy of six was brought into the department by his mother with a cut to his knee. As Joe was available to treat the child, he set about cleaning and sticking steri-strips to the boy's injury. This was during the month of December and the child was chatting about Christmas and his ideal Christmas dinner. Turning to Joe, he said "What do you have for Christmas dinner?"

Joe explained that since he had lived in England he ate turkey at Christmas, but when living in Australia had always had a barbeque on the beach with friends. Having established that his small patient did not like eating meat because he "didn't think it was fair to eat animals", Joe explained that, traditionally, turkey was not eaten for Christmas dinner on the other side of the world. This perked the young lad right up, and he announced that when he grew up he wanted to move to Australia.

Overhearing this exchange, I smiled to myself, thinking that Joe had finally got the hang of dealing with small children on their level, when I heard him ask "Well, what *do* you eat then?"

Without a moment's hesitation, Joe replied "Roo steaks".

A few seconds of silence ensued, and then "*Roo* steaks, as in KANGAroo steaks?"

"Yup" said Joe confidently, "we eat Skippy for lunch."

≈ 8 ≈

Abbreviation

All Accident and Emergency departments have their own abbreviations and mnemonics for their patients and their conditions. In the last few years, patients have had access to their medical records if requested and these abbreviations are now very rarely used in notes. They survive in the staff room, during 'handover' shift changes and, occasionally, in small letters on the whiteboard in the department.

A lot of these abbreviations are nationwide and easily transplant from hospital to hospital – most A/E departments, for example know exactly what a PAAF patient is (Pissed as a Fart), an FTF (Failure to Fly – reserved for the numerous trips and falls that we see) a WOFT (Waste of Flipping Time – for example, "I hurt my foot 6 months ago and it still hurts if I'm out jogging for more than 3 hours."!) and NPS (New Parent Syndrome – a new parent with a first child: perfectly normal child but anxious parent). Abbreviations are now very much frowned upon, and this is perfectly understandable, especially as certain abbreviations can have more than one meaning. For example, one ward or department may use "DiB" as "Dead in Bed", whereas another would use it to mean "Difficulty in Breathing", which we, in Accident and Emergency, have been known to shorten to "SOB" ("Shortness of Breath") – not to be confused with "Son of a Bitch" or "Silly Old Bag", both of which may be more appropriate at times.

We also have our 'own' monikers, probably a variation of those in other areas. The island has many small villages, a lot of which have more than a suspicion of inbreeding and resulting progeny. Some of these children can appear a little 'odd' in many subtle and varied ways and it is not unknown to see a note in a child's examination records reading "NFC – Normal for Charleston".

Chloe was 16 years old and born and bred within the village. She was brought in by a lady in her late forties, and debate between the staff as to the relationship between the two was lively; some of the staff thought that the accompanying adult was her mother, whilst Sandy, the receptionist booking them in, was convinced that granny had come with her. Knowing the village that they resided in, either was a distinct possibility. Chloe had a two day history of abdominal pain and nausea and, being sixteen years old, a certain sensitivity had to be employed in taking a history. I warned her that I would be asking her some quite personal questions and asked if she wanted to be alone with me to save embarrassment.

"No, it's ok," she said, "Cabbage can stay with me."

Well *that* was as clear as mud, and realising that I must have felt as confused as I looked, the lady accompanying Chloe explained that she was her grandmother, but when she was very young, Chloe pronounced "Granny" as "cabbage" – and the name stuck. Reception =1, nurses =0.

I continued with the history and approaching the delicate subject of sex, I first asked Chloe if she had a boyfriend.

"Oh, yes," she said "I've got loads."

Ok, that was the easy bit. I then asked if she was sexually active. Silence. I repeated that if she wished to have this conversation with me privately, then that was fine and I was sure that her grandmother would understand. (I really could not bring myself to call the lady 'Cabbage').

"No, that's ok," replied Chloe. "I'm just thinking."

To me, the question didn't really need much thinking about. Surely it was a straight 'yes' or 'no' answer.

Just as I was about to rephrase the question, I got an answer, and Chloe firmly stated that she was *not* sexually active. A good many questions later, the young girl admitted to me that she had not had a menstrual period since her "miscarriage in March". Confused, I reminded Chloe that she had told me that she was not sexually active.

"Well, I'm not exactly active." she explained. "I just lie there."

Definitely a case of 'NFC'.

Some people have a distinct ability for 'putting their foot in it' and Harriet, a junior staff nurse, was an expert. Taking over the care of a patient from the paramedics one day, she began to note the history. The middle aged lady was accompanied by her grown up son and daughter and had been admitted via her GP with a history of several unexplained collapses. The patient was not too happy about having to come into hospital and Harriet was working hard to put the lady at ease. It seemed as though there was a good rapport. Having gained an idea of the patient's immediate medical complaints, the time had come to discuss family history. The patient proceeded to tell Harriet about her husband's medical conditions, but interrupted herself to say, "Oh! But he's not a blood relative."

With a smile Harriet replied, "Unless you're from Charleston."

Dead silence… All of the family members just looked at each other.

"Don't tell me," she said, "You're from Charleston."

The patient nodded slowly.

Still silence.

Harriet busied herself rechecking the lady's blood pressure and writing the result carefully on the notes before leaving the cubicle. The kind thing to do, I suppose, would have been for another member of staff to take over the care of the patient to enable Harriet to get out of the hole that she had dug for herself – but each member of staff had their own patients *and* Harriet was assigned to the patients occupying cubicles 5–8. Her new patient was in cubicle 7 so ...

Harriet was assigned to the lady from admission to discharge. I would like to say that she learned her lesson from this and thought a little more carefully before speaking from then on, but unfortunately, this just wasn't in Harriet's nature, and the episode became just one more to add to her portfolio of cringeworthy moments.

Of course, people being people never cease to surprise us, and the triage room specialises in surprises.

Diana is a quiet and self-effacing staff nurse, not easily embarrassed, and having worked in the department for nearly ten years, had seen and heard most things. A rather demure and well groomed lady in her sixties was taken into the triage room where Diana was starting her shift. Establishing that she was there with a wrist injury, Diana proceeded to ask her how and when the injury occurred. "Well, you see," said the patient "I was having a prolonged session masturbating with a bottle last night ...."

It just goes to show that you can *never* second guess a patient, and no matter what you think – you haven't actually heard it all before!

≈ **9** ≈

Major Incident Practice

The ambulance staff work very closely with all of the other emergency services and none more so than during the annual Major Incident drills. The whole hospital has a Major Incident policy which comes into effect if there is an incident involving large amounts of people or a suspicion of chemical involvement. This is even more important on the island, as there is only one hospital and patients cannot be divided between several establishments. To transfer patients between hospitals involves the use of a helicopter and/or an hour of ferry and road travel. Hence the importance of a smooth running Major Incident plan. To ensure that this happens, every year or so a scenario is devised which involves the fire crews, police force, ambulance service and hospital.

Although the Island does not have fast motorways, there is always the possibility of somewhat more unusual incidents occurring, and scenarios have varied from a collapsing cliff cable car, to an explosion and subsequent contamination at the neighbouring oil refinery, to an overturned ferry, and once a fire at one of the major tourist attractions in the height of the summer season. These scenarios are made as realistic as possible and many members of the public are brought in as volunteer 'patients' or 'distressed relatives'. 'Real' patients in the department are given the heads up on what is about to happen as soon as the hospital is notified that a practice is imminent. Most patients take this in their stride, fully understand the necessity of the day, and are quite happy once they realise that this will not alter their treatment. Other patients are a completely different kettle of fish.

Charged with the job of explaining the Practice to the few patients in the A/E waiting room, and explaining that they might be a little longer in receiving non urgent treatment, I reminded the three women and one man that the GP surgeries were open and it would be prudent to visit their local doctor for their minor problems. As expected, two of the four patients got up to leave, and as the second patient reached the door, she turned and said "I'll pop back tomorrow then." Sometimes I feel that the words 'Accident' and 'Emergency' are not quite understood by some people!

The members of the public that volunteer for the Major Incident practices come from all walks of life and although some are slightly older, most are college students and some of these are studying drama in one form or another. These students really throw themselves into the make believe world of the incident and make very effective 'patients'. However, there is a tendency to not want their involvement to end. One of these 'patients', a young lady named Sarah, arrived at the department as 'walking wounded'. Having her 'broken arm' treated and her 'head wound' 'stitched' Sarah was officially discharged from the department and thanked for her help during the scenario. A few steps into the waiting room and Sarah began complaining of a headache and collapsed. Panic ensued amongst the real patients, relatives and the students that had ended their part in the practice, with people shouting to the staff that there was a patient on the floor in the waiting room and crowding around Sarah as she lay on the floor. Sceptical, but concerned that she really was ill, I went to her assistance and bundled her onto a trolley with help from one of the EDAs (Emergency Department Assistants).

In to the resuscitation room, and as we began to remove her top clothing in order to place a blood pressure cuff and ECG electrodes on our patient, who was not responding to us at all, we noticed that her eyelids were flickering and she had plenty of tone in her muscles, suggesting that she was not unconscious at all. In a measured tone, Benny, the EDA, stated that he was going to find the 'large bore needle' and 'rectal probe' because we were sure to need them. Amazingly, Sarah immediately opened her eyes, sat up straight and said that she really couldn't remember what had happened but she felt much better now!

If only we could fix all of our patients so quickly and effectively.

≈ 10 ≈

Nicked

Patients feigning varying degrees of illness and unconsciousness are an unfortunate and regular part of the job and can occur for a myriad of reasons. The hospital is situated in close proximity to three prisons, and there can be several patients a day from one or other of these institutions. We are always aware that some of the prison inmates may be pretending to be ill or injured in order to gain access to the hospital, and we have the safety of our staff and patients foremost in mind while the inmate is assessed. Each individual is accompanied by at least two prison officers and hand cuffed to one of them.

Artie came in from one of the prisons through the resuscitation room with a history of being found "unresponsive in his cell". Recognizing that he might be pulling a fast one, all staff were alert for signs of consciousness while undressing Artie and checking his vital signs. His pulse, blood pressure, temperature and respiratory rate were all quite normal. His heart rhythm was fine and, as we could find no sign of injury, a large cannula was placed into his vein in order to draw blood for testing and to introduce any drugs or fluids that might be necessary. Still there was no response from Artie. His muscles were quite relaxed and his breathing low and even. All of the usual pain stimuli were used in order to elicit a response but still nothing, not a flicker.

Concerned as to the cause of his condition, the senior doctor ordered a CT scan of Artie's brain. Still chained to his charge, the prison officer accompanied us to the CT room when they called that they were ready. Once Artie was placed onto the CT scanner table, and having established that he was indeed unconscious, the officer undid the handcuff and stepped into the viewing room next to the scanner. This room was between the scan room and the outer corridor and had a large glass window in order for the patient to be watched at all times. The double doors of the actual scan room were locked from the inside and a second prison officer was stationed outside them. The scan duly commenced with Artie lying completely still on the table. Just as the table was being automatically slid into the scanner, up sat our 'unconscious' patient and in one smooth movement, dropped his legs over the edge of the table, stood up and untwisted the lock to the double doors. Everyone reacted in seconds, but Artie had the element of surprise and was just a tad ahead. Somehow he dodged the prison officer guarding the doors and made off down the corridor. For an unconscious man, he could really shift!

Noticing a door leading to the outside on the left of the corridor, Artie made a beeline for it and in seconds had left the building. Unfortunately for our 'patient', he obviously hadn't studied the layout of the hospital and had quite neatly trapped himself within a small quadrangle set between the four walls of the two storey building. It was quite a simple matter for the prison officers to recapture their charge and cuff both hands, one to each officer.

Note to other intending escapees – do your homework first!

≈ 11 ≈

On the Road

Like other hospitals, we have our fair share of 'oddballs' of one sort or another, but we only get a small share of what the ambulance services on the street deal with. Being called to an emergency, two paramedics found themselves on a housing estate in an area renowned for being a bit rough. Leaving the ambulance on the road directly outside the house, the paramedics entered the home to find a large man in a dirty string vest recumbent on a sofa and complaining of "feeling dizzy". The smell of alcohol emanating from their patient was evident from the doorway and the man's slurred speech gave away the fact that he'd probably had a drink or three! Having fully examined the gentleman on his couch, the professionals concluded that far from being ill, he was simply blind drunk. The patient agreed with them and stated that he had called an ambulance because he could normally drink at least ten cans of beer before feeling any ill effects, but he'd only had eight so far and wasn't feeling too well! Reassured that he just needed to sleep it off, the patient was quite happy to remain at home and the paramedics stepped outside in order to return to their vehicle.

George and Deon were surprised to discover that their ambulance was gone! They stood at the roadside and scanned the road ahead, but their 3 tonnes of bright yellow and green van was nowhere to be seen. To his dismay, George realised that he had left the keys in the ignition when they leaped from the vehicle on their arrival. A sheepish telephone call to the police resulted in the news that an abandoned ambulance had been found half on and half off the pavement several miles down the road and an inebriated woman was seen staggering from it. Recovering the vehicle was relatively easy, but a new memo whipped around the ambulance station reminding crews to take the keys with them when they had to leave the ambulance unattended!

Not only does the ambulance service have to treat patients suffering from the effects of excessive alcohol consumption, but they are also tasked with moving some very large, morbidly obese patients from houses that they may not have left for many years. If we are to receive an obese patient from the paramedics, we are often given advance warning and we can ensure that we have a bariatric bed standing by. These beds are specially designed and built to hold patients weighing up to 350kg, with a BMI of 40 or more.

One lunchtime, a call came from ambulance control informing us that they were bringing through Mrs Tonny on the advice of her GP who was concerned about her red and inflamed right lower leg. Mrs Tonny was a very large lady, with her weight estimated at well over 159 kg/25 stone. One of the senior staff nurses received Mrs Tonny from the ambulance crew on her arrival and she was quickly transferred onto the bariatric bed. Rachel began undressing her new patient and called for a hand from another member of staff to help remove the voluminous slip that she was wearing. As the slip was lifted over her head, Rachel noticed an object nestled within the folds of her ample bosom. Holding the ends of the object, she removed it to find a ball point pen. Not just any ball point pen, but a novelty pen with a pink fluffy end. Mrs Tonny was delighted with her 'new' acquisition – apparently

she liked to do crosswords in bed and was constantly losing
her pens.

≈ 12 ≈

Pop Festival

One of the unique aspects of being the only A/E unit on the island is the annual Pop Festival. The staff of St Josephs is called upon to staff the emergency tents stationed beside the main stage. The advantage, of course, is a free pass to the festival, but this is tempered by the fact that it is nigh on impossible to hear anything through a stethoscope – and you can almost guarantee to be thrown up on and/or urinated on at some point!

The Festival takes place over four days, and during that time the Accident and Emergency tents will treat two to three hundred patients. The majority of these are over indulgence of alcohol, allergies/asthma and dehydration, but there is always 'something different'. Just half an hour into my shift one Saturday, I was asked to step outside the tent to treat a young lady with an established history of well controlled epilepsy. She was in the throes of a seizure, but before today had been seizure free on medication for over three years. Recovering, the lass informed me that her medication shouldn't be mixed with alcohol as it increased the risk of seizures, and so she had made the deliberate decision to drink alcohol and forgo her medication. She was quite convinced that her choice was a good one and was a little upset that it hadn't quite gone to plan.

A couple of hours later, a man staggered into the tent rather the worse for wear and half naked. Trying vainly to get some sort of history from him, it appeared that he had lost his shirt somewhere in the field and wanted someone to phone his mum to bring him a new one. He couldn't remember his mother's phone number and anyway, hadn't got a phone with him. Having established that the gentleman was not injured in any way, we guided him out of the tent to try and find the friends that he had come to the festival with. He had remembered that they were staying in a green tent, so we knew that he had his work well and truly cut out – there were over a thousand tents out there and approximately half of them were green. We didn't have any intention of phoning his mum for him and disturbing her weekend, as his mother lived many miles away on the mainland and, anyway, the man was at least in his mid-thirties!

The biggest inconvenience for festival goers at all of the big festivals, whether it be Glastonbury, Reading, the Isle of Wight or anywhere else in the country, is the 'conveniences' themselves. No matter how many port-a-loos there are at a festival, there are never enough, and huge queues form for the dubious pleasure of using one of these small, ultra smelly plastic cubicles. Having worked at the festival site over several years, I have seen and treated a good few people who have had 'accidents' of one sort or another while answering the call of nature.

I suppose the worst of these had to be a young lady brought into the tent smelling strongly of excrement and in the throes of a major panic attack. She was escorted by one of the security officers who had been called over to help by the girl's friends. Apparently she had been stuck in one of the cubicles and had to be extricated by several security officers with a pair of wicked looking bolt cutters.

After half an hour of rest and a glass of cold water, she had calmed down a little, and explained what had happened. Apparently when pulling down her jeans, her new iPhone had fallen out of her back pocket and into the toilet. Before removing her jeans, she had not noticed that the flushing mechanism of that particular toilet was not working, but as soon as she heard her mobile phone land in the WC with a resounding 'plop' she turned around to see it rapidly sinking into a sea of human waste. Now, personally, I would have cursed my bad luck and accepted that my phone was gone forever, but not so this plucky lass. Instead, she knelt down on the dirty floor and plunged her arm up to the elbow into the smelly lavatory. Scrabbling around, she was just able to touch the hard edge of the phone. Leaning forward, she pushed her arm further into the toilet and finally managed to grasp the edge of the phone, but, in doing so suddenly became aware that she could no longer extricate her arm. Determined not to let her phone slip from her grasp, she hung onto it and, still kneeling in a puddle of goodness knows what, began calling to her friends for help. Luckily, her friends waiting outside heard her and, as the door was locked, called the security guys over, thinking that she had locked herself in. By the time that security had forced open the door, the young lass had been sitting on the sodden floor with her arm shoulder deep in a pile of excrement for some fifteen minutes.

While she was waiting, a combination of the revolting smell and the realisation of exactly what she had her hand and arm in resulted in hyperventilation and a full blown panic attack. Luckily, the girl was an island resident and not camping, and could therefore return home for a shower. Had she been camping in a small two or three person tent then she might well have found that she had that tent all to herself that night!

≈ 13 ≈

To Phone...or Not to Phone?

In the fast moving Accident and Emergency department one of the most frustrating things is trying to complete a mountain of paperwork before the patient can be released to a ward. The multitude of forms to fill in can guarantee at least one or two time consuming telephone calls from the general public.

Back to Christmas Day, which seems to bring out all sorts of odd behaviour in people. I answered the telephone while trying to finish the notes for two different patients. The lady on the other end asked me if we were having a busy day and if we were managing to have a nice Christmas, despite the fact that we were all working. I answered that we were doing our best and asked her why she was ringing, did she have a problem?

"Yes," she said "I have a really big problem."

Reassuring her that I would do my best to help her, I asked her to explain what the problem was.

After spending a while explaining that she normally lived alone, but today she had a 'houseful of relatives for dinner', she asked me how long she should cook her Christmas turkey.

Taking a deep breath, I asked if *that* was her problem.

Apparently it was, and I informed her that this was not exactly an Accident or Emergency problem and to read a cook book.

Quick as a flash, she answered back that if she didn't cook it properly then the whole family would become ill with food poisoning, would have to attend A/E, and it would *become* my problem.

I handed the phone to Debbie, who was sitting next to me. She calmly told the caller that twenty minutes per pound should do it! The lady hung up quite satisfied, and I quietly admired Debbie for taking the call so calmly.

≈ 14 ≈

Come Fly with Me

Emergency patients requiring specialist care are transferred from St Joseph's to specialist hospitals. One of the more common transfers is by helicopter to the nearest Neurological Centre for those trauma patients with head injuries. Some members of staff are more enthusiastic about a helicopter trip than others, but no matter who goes, the very first transfer that you participate in is always fraught with anxiety. Every patient is accompanied by piles of paperwork as well as various pieces of equipment and medication, and it is quite a feat of organisational skill to ensure that everything is present and correct in time.

Dominic had been working in the department for several years when it was decided that his patient needed to be transferred across the sea. Not having flown before (not even on an aeroplane on holiday), Dominic was very excited about his very first helicopter trip, and busied himself preparing his patient for the journey. His patient was the driver of a car involved in a road traffic collision and had head and spinal injuries. Dominic, being a very confident and thorough nurse, had everything up together, had kept the relatives of his patient fully informed, liaised with the accepting unit, and was fully prepared for the transfer.

After leaving the department, Dominic was gone for several hours – as is the norm for helicopter transfers – for although the trip takes a short time by air, the accompanying staff all have to make the return journey by ferry, along with most of the equipment that they have taken with them.

On his return, the rest of the staff were anxious to know how he had got on and were a little non-plussed at Dominic's comment merely that it was "ok". Further questioning of the doctor that had flown with them revealed that in fact Dominic had turned rather green shortly after take-off and had spent most of the short journey vomiting! Although he had started the trip full of enthusiasm, it rather appeared that Dominic's nursing career was destined to be confined to looking after his patients on terra firma.

≈ 15 ≈

Spiders!

Most people have a fear of *something* and I am quite open and honest about my own phobia of spiders. This is a real life, gut wrenching phobia, as opposed to a simple dislike: and at times it can be a serious disadvantage.

As a teenager I shared a flat with several friends in a large Victorian house which had been divided into three fairly big flats. One morning, alone in the flat, I stripped off in my bedroom and padded naked down the hall to the bathroom. Turning on both of the bath taps, I bent down to put the plug in the hole – and I heard a distinct thud. Turning my head to one side I came face to face with the largest, hairiest spider I had ever seen in my life. I shot upright, lost my footing and landed butt first on the hard tiled floor.

As I landed, my head snapped back and momentum bounced it off the floor. Dazed and bleeding from a wound on the back of the head, my main priority was to escape before the spider figured out where I had gone and came to get me. I staggered to my feet and fled from the bathroom.

Not quite thinking straight, I realised that I needed help because I wasn't sure of how badly injured I was (there seemed to be an awful lot of blood) and I wanted that spider GONE. Not just gone, but <u>deceased</u> and gone so that it didn't come back.

Our landline telephone was not working at the time and my flat was the top floor of the house, reached by an iron staircase on the outside of the building. Without thinking, I flung open the front door and ran down the steps heading for the ground floor flat where a married couple, Karen and Sean, lived. I knew that *their* telephone was working and I intended to call one of my flat mates to ask them to come home and help me out. The outer steps were cold on my feet and it was only when I had almost reached the bottom that I remembered that I was totally starkers! I immediately turned around and ran back up the steps, into the spider infested flat! The minor injury to my head had stopped bleeding by now, and as I passed the full length mirror in the hall I took stock of my appearance. Naked, pale, with blood matted hair and a blood stained neck – I looked a fright.

Edging towards the still open bathroom door, I pulled the door shut so that the revolting arachnid was trapped. I had to leave the bath taps running because there was no way I was going any closer to the bath. I got dressed and then made a more controlled journey downstairs.

The house was situated on a busy main road, with the iron staircase fully visible from the front. It was just past ten o'clock on a weekday morning and the street was busy with pedestrians: mothers pushing prams, single people and couples, with cyclists and motorists constantly passing by on the road. I can't imagine that my first hurried descent had been entirely unnoticed and the fact that I had been neither approached by a member of the public nor visited by the police was possibly something to do with being in the centre of a Birmingham suburb! That was not the first time that a spider had got the better of me, and certainly wouldn't be the last.

All of the wards in St Joseph's Hospital, with the exception of the Medical Assessment Unit, are situated on the first or second floors (levels B and C – A being the ground floor) and are reached by one of two lifts. One autumn day, I was walking along the corridor beside a trolley conveying my elderly patient to the lift in order to reach the orthopaedic ward. The trolley was being pushed by two of the hospital porters, and my patient was chatting away about her impending surgery to repair her fractured hip. As we entered the lift, I squeezed myself in beside the trolley and just as the doors began to close, happened to glance downward to see a large spider climbing up the side of the trolley towards the patient's feet. Consider: we were in a confined space and I really do not care for these creatures at all. Consequently I dived out of the lift door, abandoning my patient completely.

This came as a complete shock to the porters, who were on the way up in the lift with the patient before they digested the fact that I had gone. The patient herself was facing the rear of the lift car and was still nattering away, not realising that I was no longer with her! Now safe from a spider attack, I did a very fast walk back down the corridor to the main staircase and ran up the two flights to floor B. Another fast walk down that corridor and to another two flights of stairs leading to the topmost floor where the orthopaedic ward was, my patient's intended destination. Luckily, the lift containing the patient and porters had been stopped halfway up at level B, where a couple of people had squeezed into the lift to go up to orthopaedics. So by the time that I caught up with the trolley, and patient, they had only just arrived on the ward. Red faced and puffing with exertion, I tried very much to get my act together in order to hand the patient over to the ward staff, at the same time making a mental note to get fit.

I took my time helping the elderly lady onto her bed and ensuring that she was comfortable while willing my heart rate to slow down. By the time that the ward staff was ready for the hand over, I was breathing more evenly and my pulse rate had neared my normal level. Not a single member of staff queried my abrupt arrival on the ward, or my red faced appearance, and I was certainly not about to try and explain my rather odd behaviour. I swore the porters to secrecy and never did admit to abandoning a helpless little old lady with a fractured hip in a lift on the way to the ward.

≈ 16 ≈

Stuck Up

One of the first things that people say when I tell them where I work is "I bet you've seen some odd things stuck in weird places," and yes, I can truly say that some incidents really beggar belief.

A call came through from the ambulance service informing the department that they were bringing in a gentleman with abdominal pain. Details were a little sketchy until the aforementioned gentleman arrived.

He was certainly in a lot of discomfort and was lying on his side on the ambulance trolley. Although he *did* have abdominal pain, and lots of it, his primary complaint was the foreign object in his rectum. According to the patient, he was 'playing around' with his friend – who had not accompanied him to the hospital – and his 'friend' had inserted a butternut squash into the patient's rectum. The large bowel is quite elastic and when stretched to accommodate a mass, is inclined to produce waves of strong peristaltic action. This movement of the bowel had, in effect, sucked the fruit further into the bowel and out of reach. When the unfortunate gentleman realised that he could not remove the offending fruit, and began to get overwhelming abdominal cramps, he thought that he might need medical help.

There was not a lot that could be done in the emergency department to help the patient. He ended up requiring major surgery and repairs to his damaged bowel. On hearing that the offending item was a butternut squash, the first reaction of most people was "no way, too big," but lo and behold, when telephoning theatre after his surgery, it appeared that they *had* removed a medium sized peanut shaped butternut squash from within the patient's large bowel! Funnily enough, following that incident, a good few members of staff stopped eating the fruit altogether, and I, for one, have never bought one since!

≈ 17 ≈

What's Love Got to do with it?

As part of the training of junior doctors, they are required to rotate through the Accident and Emergency department, usually staying for six months at a time. These dedicated men and women come in all shapes, sizes and nationalities and young, single, good looking male doctors are always particularly appreciated by the young, single, (usually) female staff.

Nick came to work with us one August, having just finished his stint on the medical unit. Good looking, tall, and blonde – he was quickly deemed a good catch. Alice, one of the staff nurses, was one of the first in the department to meet Nick, and was determined to have him notice her. She tried to arrange it so that he was the doctor to see her allocated patients as often as possible, and even offered to do other nurses' shifts in the resuscitation room so that she could work closely with him. Nick didn't seem to pick up on these non-verbal cues, but Alice wasn't daunted.

Although she was trying so hard to catch his attention, Alice didn't quite have the nerve to ask him outright for a date, but as he was staying around until February of the following year, she was hoping that 'the subtle approach' would pay off.

A few weeks into Nick's rotation, Alice was on her way to the doctor's office with a request for a prescription when she took a couple of minutes out to nip to the staff toilet. Diving in to the small cubicle for a quick wee the overwhelming smell hit her – someone with a large problem had obviously just vacated the room. Already being there, and desperate to go, she held her breath, did what she needed to do and, flinging the door open, dived out ...... bumping straight into Nick who was waiting to go in.

Feeling the need to vindicate herself, she stammered "that wasn't me!"

"What wasn't?" asked Nick.

"The smell, that wasn't me, I didn't do it."

As Alice heard herself speak she realised that by saying what she did, when she did, she probably made things worse, and so giving a wan smile she sidled past and kept out of Nick's way for the rest of the shift.

A few days later, hoping that the incident was forgotten, Alice was sitting at the nurse's desk writing notes when Ross came and stood behind her. Ross was an Emergency Nurse Practitioner, a senior member of the nursing staff and had a warped sense of humour. Just as she became aware of Ross' presence, Nick also appeared at the front of the desk and leaned over to pick up a copy of his patients notes. Quietly, Ross broke wind and subtly waved the evil smell towards the front of the desk with the papers he had in his hand – and then, smirking, walked away. Nick straightened up, took a single sniff and then hurriedly left for the safety of the doctors' office.

Needless to say, Alice went without her date, and Nick completed his rotation blissfully unaware of her infatuation.

≈ 18 ≈

You've got a What in your Where?

Sometimes, it is a language or culture difference that causes a problem. One perfectly ordinary week day morning a young lady came into the department. This young lady had been advised to attend Accident and Emergency with the intention of seeking a surgical opinion from a specialist. It was quite common practice for various specialities to use Accident and Emergency as a 'first stop' for their patients needing possible admission. Here, they would be admitted by the Accident and Emergency staff and assessed by the speciality that had accepted their care from the GP. Then either a bed on the required ward would be found, or the patient discharged home with advice and/or medication. This kind of work forms a large chunk of the working day, and when Miss Davis arrived clutching her GP referral letter, it was just one more patient 'for the surgeons'. After being examined by a member of the surgical team, it was decided to admit Miss Davis for observation.

This is the point at which the paperwork really begins. One part of this is the listing, in triplicate, of the property and valuables that the patient is bringing into hospital with them. The reason for this is twofold: firstly, it ensures that the property brought into hospital with the patient is recorded and this is then checked regularly while the patient is in hospital to ensure that nothing goes missing. Secondly, and just as importantly, it ensures that no-one is accused of making off with an item that a patient claims that they brought with them. Usually, this is simply a case of misunderstanding when a patient thinks that they have something with them, but after reaching a hospital ward realises that they can't find it and reports it as lost or stolen, when in actual fact it is still sitting on the kitchen table at home. There have been cases in the past though, when patients have claimed that they had thousands of pounds or a diamond encrusted Rolex watch when they entered hospital, and as they no longer had it, it must have been stolen!

The tedious filling out of the property forms put paid to this kind of incident and helps to reassure the patient that their fifty year old wedding band or the Christening bracelet that they've worn since they were a baby, is safe. Every single non-clothing item is recorded on the forms, and, with more and more men as well as women wearing jewellery and having various parts of the body pierced with studs and rings, the time taken to complete the forms takes longer and longer.

Ingrid is a German Emergency Department Assistant (EDA), and, although she has been in the UK for well over twenty years, still has a strong German accent and at times, finds various English phrases and words confusing. More often than not, it was the EDAs that ended up filling in the dreaded property forms and Ingrid probably did more than her fair share.

Miss Davis was no stranger to the body piercer's needle and had at least half a dozen earrings in each ear. With her nose piercing and the stud in her tongue, I could hear Ingrid adding up the tally as she went. Finally adding the last one Ingrid asked her patient "is that it?"

"All except for the clitoral ring," she said.

After a heartbeat of silence, I heard Ingrid exclaim "A what?"

"A ring in my clitoris."

"You have a WHAT in your WHERE?"

By their very nature, A/E departments aren't very private places and patients are only divided from each other by flimsy curtains – and unfortunately Ingrid's voice tended to rise in volume by a tone or two when she was confused or startled. Consequently almost the entire department had gone quiet and was listening to the conversation. The whole effect was made more comical by Ingrid's strong accent, so the question came out more as "You have a VOT in your VERE?"!

Miss Davis, seemingly unconcerned, simply repeated that she had a piercing "down there."

"Your VORGINA is pierced?" asked Ingrid "VHY?"

At this point, Ellen decided to rescue both Ingrid and the patient, and went into the cubicle to continue with the paperwork herself, but poor Ingrid never could understand why a person would want to have their private parts pierced, and, even more mind-boggling, who did the piercing?

Miss Davis was not the only patient that we saw with a 'private' piercing.

Kirsty and Simon attended the department together, both on the same ambulance stretcher and partly dressed, covered by an ambulance issue blanket. Arriving in the side room, they moved gingerly from the ambulance trolley, again together, and with a bit of prompting, gave the reason for attendance.

It appeared that in order to spice up their sex life, both Kirsty and Simon had had their genitalia pierced, with Kirsty sporting a clitoris ring, and Simon with a 'Prince Albert' – a hoop piercing that went through the urethra and emerged beneath the glans of his penis. Both ends of the hoop terminated in a ball bearing that were on a screw thread. Kirsty's body adornment was also a hoop, but with a small blue glass jewel set within the loop. Unfortunately, whilst in the throes of passion, the 'ball' of Simons piercing had become firmly stuck within the hoop of Kirsty's piercing, jamming behind the 'jewel'. Thus stuck, passion had cooled rapidly as they desperately tried to 'unhook' themselves. The more they pushed and pulled to try to untangle themselves, the more painful both piercings became, with the eventual result that both partners began bleeding.

Seeing the damage, and beginning to panic, the pair sized up their options. They decided against calling friends or family for help and debated whether to call the fire service instead, as Simon could recall how helpful they had been when his younger brother had got his hand caught in a grate a few years previously!

Eventually, they came to the decision to call an ambulance as they thought that the paramedics might carry equipment to cut the rings off and no-one else need know. Instead, both of the injured parties were taken, by ambulance, into the Accident and Emergency department full of people! The paramedics were concerned about the bleeding and the fact that there could be damage to vital parts.

Carefully examining both parties, it was apparent that the sensitive tissues were continuing to swell and the bleeding from both piercings was making the field quite difficult to visualise. Eventually, having decided that the ring cutters would cause more harm than good, the doctor treating the pair managed to grasp the 'ball' on one end of the 'Prince Albert' with a pair of forceps and, holding the ring with another pair began twisting carefully until he could remove the ball and slide the bar from the body of Simon and through Kirsty's ring. A double prescription of anti-inflammatories later and the couple were able to make their way home via a lift from a friend – although chances are they never gave their friend the *exact* reason for their visit.

≈ 19 ≈

Living on an Island

Before moving from mainland Britain and onto this small island just off the coast, I have to confess to not knowing exactly where the island was positioned in the British Isles. I am not alone in my ignorance but before actually working on the Island, I wasn't aware of just how widespread this ignorance was. It is certainly not a rare occurrence to find a prospective visitor phoning to ask if they have to bring their passport with them when they are coming to see their relative in hospital. However, a gentleman from Lincolnshire topped that quite easily when I telephoned him to tell him that his elderly mother had been admitted to hospital and would be requiring surgery in the next couple of days.

Mrs Snow was a little old lady of eighty two who had come on her first holiday to the Island with her equally elderly friend and neighbour. Both ladies lived in sheltered accommodation in Birmingham and had come to the island on a coach trip to enjoy the fresh air and sea breezes just a day earlier. Unfortunately, alighting from her coach that afternoon, Mrs Snow had stumbled and fallen, breaking her left hip in the process.

As she was due to be admitted to the orthopaedic ward later on that evening, I phoned her son, who was also her next of kin, to inform him of his mother's accident and impending admission. When he asked if it would be alright to come down and visit her, I answered that she would like that as she was quite frightened and had hoped that he would do so.

Approximately five minutes after ending the call, the phone rang and it was Mr Snow – he had forgotten that his passport was out of date and wondered if I knew where he could obtain an emergency passport that day. I reassured him that we were actually part of the United Kingdom and were only a couple of miles away from the mainland coast, across a short stretch of sea. Seemingly satisfied, he said that he would be leaving within the next half hour and would phone when he reached the ferry. Mrs Snow was delighted that her son was coming down to visit her, especially as he had never been south of Birmingham in his entire life!

An hour or so later, the phone on the nurse's desk rang again and one of the nurses handed it to me saying "it's Mr Snow". Expecting that he had phoned to gain an update on his mother's condition, I took the phone from her.

Indeed it *was* Mr Snow on the other end, but instead of ringing to see how Mrs Snow was coping, he was nearly in tears and asked me to relay a message to say that he wouldn't be coming to see her today at all. Concerned, I asked if he was ok, only for him to reply that yes, he was fine, but the post office was shut and therefore he couldn't get his currency changed – and without exchanging his money, he couldn't pay for food or accommodation in Island currency!

≈ 20 ≈

Further Education

S tudy days and courses come in two types, and whilst some are for continuing and furthering education, others are mandatory and have to be repeated each year. One of the latter is Manual Handling, the art of shifting patients from A to B using all manner of hoists and apparatus, and is a boring but necessary annual update. Another, less desirable course is the day devoted to food hygiene. The Hospital Trust states that if staff is providing food of any sort, then they have to be educated on the dangers of not storing and handling food correctly. As a department, we were not providing meals per se but as we did provide some patients with cups of tea and, when needed, a slice or two of toast, this meant that we fell into the category of 'providing food' and hence all staff were required to attend the food hygiene course to ensure that we did not inadvertently poison our charges.

Diana, our manager, was a stickler for making sure that the staff attended these days and would put a list on the wall of the staff room highlighting who needed to go on what course and when. I noticed that my name had cropped up on the food hygiene course more than once, but to be honest, I couldn't see the point of spending a day in a classroom being educated on the merits of 'sell by' dates, and the consequences of serving furry food to patients. I had managed to bring up three children and live to the ripe age of forty-something without poisoning anyone in the kitchen, was quite proficient at spotting mouldy bread and could think of much better things to do with my time.

Noticing that I hadn't attended the course for nearly eighteen months, Diana made a point of putting my name on the list for the next course and then pulled me aside to tell me that I was attending it whether I liked it or not. I tried to explain the futility of such a wasted day, but Diana was insistent – it was Trust policy and if I didn't show up, then it was a disciplinary offence. Slyly, I mentioned that I hadn't been feeling 100% well lately and it would be an awful shame if I was ill and missed the course. A withering look from my manager said it all, and I knew there would be trouble if I dared to 'pull a sickie'.

Luckily, I wasn't alone in attending the course that day and I knew that Megan, another staff nurse from the department, would be keeping me company. Megan was a conscientious nurse and was quite happy to attend these courses if that was what policy dictated: they might be boring, but they were a necessary evil!

Unfortunately, on the morning of the course, I woke up feeling dreadful – dizzy, with a headache and blurred vision. I couldn't believe it: here I was feeling ill and I had to go and sit in a stuffy classroom and listen to someone telling me how to wash up kitchen utensils properly and not serve anything that has been previously dropped on the floor! I thought of phoning the course director to explain that I was too ill to attend, but the image of my manager's face and the words 'disciplinary offence' rose before me.

Cursing my big mouth, I made my way to the classrooms in the hospital grounds, meeting up with Megan on the way. I opened my mouth to explain that I was feeling unwell, but she got in first. She took one look at me and said 'you look dreadful!' I told her that I would have cancelled the day, but had already threatened to 'pull a sickie' and it was a well-known fact that I really did not want to attend the course. Far from being sympathetic, Megan said 'you'll just have to go then.'

From the moment that we arrived in the classroom I knew that attending had been a big mistake. The classroom was small and stuffy, with small windows that did not open. The lecturer's voice was dull and uninteresting and I found myself constantly fighting sleep. My desk was placed next to Megan and every few moments she prodded me awake, or pushed me upright in my seat. The room wasn't particularly full, and every time that the lecturer looked towards me, Megan had to employ a distraction technique to avoid him noticing that I was half asleep and not really on the same planet. The course lasted a full day and somehow I got through it. It was noted on the staff room list that I attended, although if asked, I could recall absolutely none of the content of the day, and Megan was mentally exhausted and felt as though she'd done a full day on 'the shop floor'.

≈ 21 ≈

On-Line Self Help

Patients attending the Accident and Emergency department as 'walking wounded' first need to stop by the reception desk and book themselves in as a patient. Here, they give their basic details and the reason for their attendance. Consequently, the two receptionists, Sandy and Marta have seen and heard many weird and wonderful things over their time. Marta came back to the desk having just finished her coffee break to find a young man shifting uneasily from foot to foot on the other side of the counter.

Marta: "Hello, how can I help?"

Patient: "Um. I think I have an STI."

Marta: "What symptoms do you have that makes you think that?"

Patient: "Well, I don't really know. My computer told me to be here."

Marta: "Are you feeling unwell?"

Patient: "No. I'm not sure. I just need to see a doctor – now!"

Marta: "Are you registered with a GP? Maybe they would be the best person to speak to."

At this point, the patient became quite agitated and insisted that he had come to the hospital to see a doctor that didn't know him. Apparently, the family GP was a friend of his father and he didn't want his father to know that he had a sexually transmitted disease. Trying to calm the young man down, and to get an idea of his symptoms, Marta explained that there was no problem, she could arrange for a doctor to see him in Accident and Emergency if he wished, but needed to know what made him think that he needed to see a doctor, as she had to record *something* in the box on her screen under 'presenting complaint'.

"Well," said the patient, "I was looking at some porn stuff last night online and this morning I turned my computer on and it told me I have a virus!"

Many patients these days turn to their computer before going to see a doctor, and I know that I'm not alone in supressing a sigh when a patient sits down in the triage room, pulls a bit of paper from his pocket and proceeds to tell me his list of symptoms, followed by the diagnosis, and then requests certain medication or treatment for his problem either because that is what 'the internet said' or because he 'Googled it'.

Calling Ruth from the waiting room into the triage room, my heart sank as the inevitable piece of creased paper appeared from her pocket as she sat down.

"I know what it is," she said as soon as she sat down.

"How about we start at the beginning," I replied. "Tell me what's brought you here to A/E?"

Smoothing the piece of paper out on her knee, she jabbed her finger at each point as she read down the list.

"Number 1, I've been getting pain low down in my belly.

"Number 2, I've been feeling odd –sometimes I feel hot and cold."

At this point I'm wracking my brains for the myriad of things that could cause these vague symptoms and Ruth continued –

"Every now and then I feel a bit sick and – what gave it away – is that I sometimes find it hard to pee, and when I do it hurts."

Having a better idea now, and reaching into the cupboard for a sample pot so that I can ask for a sample of urine, Ruth continued,

"I told you – I know what it is," she said "I phoned my GP but she can't see me until Friday and I need treatment now."

Folding up her bit of paper, she looked me squarely in the eye and said:

"It's my prostrate!"

There is nothing more demoralising than putting your head into the waiting room on a busy day to find that it is still heaving with patients, no matter how many you have already seen. Weekends are the worst, and the in-joke in the department is that the A/E unit is on the tourist board's 'places to visit' list. One Saturday, I am quite sure that a particular lady had read this 'list'. She came in with her seven children, plus her sister and her sister's four children and wanted EVERYONE to be seen.

Apparently they had all been to a picnic on the mainland two weeks ago with her brother, who was diagnosed as having MRSA (Methicillin-resistant Staphylococcus aureus: a 'superbug') in a wound a week later by his local hospital. There were absolutely no signs or symptoms of anything in anyone, no-one had an open wound and the children, ranging in age from a toddler to a sullen looking twelve or thirteen year old, were milling around in the waiting room. The lady booking them in said that she wanted everyone to be seen by a doctor: she was insistent about "wanting to be checked out" and really couldn't understand when Sandy said that, although we never turn anyone away from Accident and Emergency, it would probably be better to arrange to see her own GP in the week where she could make individual appointment times.

The lady wasn't having any of that. She stated that she had gone to the effort of collecting all the children together on a

Saturday so that they could all come together and so that none of them would be missing any school. Sandy gave up and went to fetch Terry, the nurse in charge that day. He carefully took the lady to one side and explained that her 'problem' did not fit into the definition of an Accident or an Emergency and that if she really needed the whole family to be seen, she had to phone her health visitor or her GP during the week. As she left – taking her entourage with her – the waiting room suddenly emptied and the day began to look a lot easier.

≈ 22 ≈

Getting Plastered

As the years have gone by, the Accident and Emergency Unit has become more and more busy, as has the rest of the hospital and, in fact, all A/E departments and hospital wards throughout the country. We no longer have the time available which, in my first few years of working in the department, the senior nurses would utilise by each taking a subject and – during a few quiet moments – providing an impromptu teaching session for the rest of the staff.

Gordon is a senior nurse and one of the more experienced plaster technicians. During one quiet afternoon, he decided to teach a small group of junior staff how to apply a long leg backslab plaster. These are particularly awkward plasters to apply as the whole leg has to be held in position whilst the plaster of Paris is applied to the back of the full leg only, and then bandaged in position. Having picked a slightly unwilling volunteer from among the more junior staff, Gordon proceeded to apply the plaster, explaining the procedure as he went. The whole process took approximately twenty minutes and when he was done, the junior member of staff was sporting a lovely plaster cast from her thigh down to her toes.

Having finished his demonstration, Gordon instructed the other three members of staff to get some more rolls of plaster and other necessary equipment to apply their own plasters. Just as they were about to start, the cardiac arrest alarm went off as a patient in the Majors side of the department arrested. A nurse shoved her head in the plaster room, asked Gordon to assist and then disappeared again.

Gordon dashed into Majors to help out, leaving the junior staff in the plaster room, not quite sure what to do. A few moments later, they followed Gordon to Majors to see if they could be of assistance, while alone on the bed in the plaster room sat Gemma, with her left leg fully encased in a rapidly hardening plaster cast. After another ten minutes or so, during which the rest of the staff were rushing around busily, a little face appeared at the edge of the plaster room as Gemma asked "Could someone help me get this off please?"

≈ 23 ≈

By Phone

The telephone is the first point of contact for some patients. Sometimes the patient just needs a little advice on how to deal with their problem; at other times they are advised to come in and visit so that they can be seen and treated. Having answered the phone twice within as many minutes and advised people on very minor ailments, Meryl pushed the phone in my direction the next time it rang.

Before I had time to speak, the voice from the other end said "I think I broke my arm, and I need someone to come here and check it out."

I explained to the lady caller that she was quite welcome to come to A/E for us to look at it.

Patient: "If I come up there will I get home in time to watch EastEnders?"

I seemed to remember that EastEnders started on the BBC at about 7.30pm and it was now six o'clock in the evening. I told the patient that once she arrived, we would see and treat her in as quick a time as we could, but the length of time that she would be in the department depended partly on the amount of patients in the department at the time, and, more crucially, on exactly what was wrong with her arm. While I was in the middle of explaining the process to her, the patient interrupted with "Can you just send someone to my house to check it out?"

Patiently I explained that she had actually called A/E and not the ambulance service and that we don't make house calls from the Accident and Emergency department.

"I know who I called!" said the patient, "but EastEnders is on soon, and last time I came up to A/E I had to wait for hours. I missed it on Monday, so I've got to see it tonight. Don't you care about your patients? Come over here and check me out."

Resisting the impulse to just hang up, I repeated that if she would like to come up to the hospital we would be happy to check on her arm and x-ray it if necessary. We would then treat it accordingly. A moment or two of silence ensued, in which I presumed the patient was working out how to get to A/E from wherever she was calling from, and then finally she spoke.

"Don't bother then," she said "if it falls off I'll sue. I need to find out who killed Archie."

We never did have a lady with a suspected broken arm come in, either that day or the next, and so I can only assume that the offending limb *didn't* drop off due to her watching her favourite soap.

Sometimes the telephone calls are really obscure. The receptionist on duty the following day told me that she had received a telephone call from a patient saying that he was diabetic and needed someone to go and get him a McDonald's burger and large fries. Apparently he had no food in the house and couldn't take his Metformin tablet without a meal!

≈ 24 ≈

Night Shift

Being a 24 hour facility, the hospital needs to be staffed throughout the entire day and night. Night shifts are never popular, although they do seem to suit some staff better than others. In St Joseph's, once the evening staff have gone home, the main hospital doors and the doors to the A/E department are locked. There is a buzzer and intercom beside the door and anyone needing to come in can ring the buzzer.

One night nearing midnight the door buzzer rang and an elderly gentleman was heard panting through the intercom "It's my wife, she can't breathe."

Two members of staff went running down the corridor, one pushing a wheelchair, in order to open the door and collect the wife. When the double doors were opened, there stood the gentleman and beside him, a sprightly looking elderly lady muffled up against the cold. The gentleman propelled his wife forward and into the waiting wheelchair.

"Is this your wife, sir?" asked one of the nurses, "I thought you said she can't breathe?"

"She can't!" he said. "She's had a bunged up nose for nearly a week and she can't breathe through it at all!"

Why a midnight visit to Accident and Emergency was necessary for a week old cold I really don't know, but the reasoning of some people defies logic.

There is no singular 'type' of patient that attends Accident and Emergency for weird and wonderful reasons, although, in my experience, it is those of the general populace that are under the age of thirty that are more likely to roll up with complaints that cause a moment's pause and a raised eyebrow, especially in the wee hours.

Although we see many of these patients, the ambulance service attends many, many more. Just last week one of the paramedics was asked to attend a house party where a 22 year old non-smoking male was out with his friends. He had smoked 2 cigarettes, felt dizzy and short of breath, and called an ambulance. Needless to say, he didn't get as far as the Accident and Emergency department, and was given a stern lecture on the dangers of smoking into the bargain!

Although the rota was arranged so each member of staff works some days and some nights, there are certain individuals that request night shifts as a preference. I can truly say that I've never quite understood this, as I've found night shifts to be a sanctioned form of torture. I would much prefer to be working during relatively 'normal' daylight hours and sleeping with the rest of the world, at night.

Erin was one of those odd people that preferred nights. She was a senior staff nurse in her late fifties and was nearing retirement. Erin had worked almost permanent night shifts for a good many years and was very much of the 'old school'. She was a staunch Catholic grandmother from Dublin and if any patient was unfortunate enough to die on her shift, Erin would go around the entire department opening all of the windows to allow the patient's 'soul to fly'. All very well in the summer months, but in the dead of winter at 2am, it rendered some parts of the department akin to a walk-in freezer.

Erin stood for no nonsense from patients and staff alike, and many a time she has sent a young house officer back to the doctor's office with his tail between his legs because of an illegible prescription or incomplete set of notes.

Each hospital has its regular attenders, or 'frequent flyers' and St Joseph's is no exception. Having been in the same department for many years, Erin knew most of them – and the time wasters always got short shrift.

A lady in her mid-twenties came in at one o'clock in the morning. She was well known to the department and usually came in when she had a crisis in her life. Susan was not only well known to the A/E unit, but was a regular at the local police station too. More often than not, she came in in various stages of inebriation, the amount of alcohol consumed usually proportional to her current crisis. This time she came in saying that she had been having "seizures all day".

Most of us had witnessed Susan's 'seizures' at one time or another, and they usually consisted of her flopping her arms by her sides and moving her head from side to side with her eyes tightly closed, whilst fully conscious and aware. This time, she walked into the department, booked herself in, and then said that she needed a doctor to pronounce her unfit for her court appearance the next morning. The doctor on duty had a quick look at her and, pronouncing her as fit as anyone could be on seven or eight cans of cheap beer, discharged her home. "But I can't go home," she said, "I need a sick note. I've been having seizures – look!"

And with that she slid gently to the floor (avoiding the sharp edges of the cabinet right next to her) and began waving her head and arms around.

Susan had picked the wrong night to come in, for Erin was over in a flash and standing next to her said "If I were you young lady, I'd get my feckin ass off the floor right now, before I shove you into a corner out of everybody's way."

Susan's erratic movements slowed for a moment while she pondered this, and then resumed.

"Right that's it." Erin hauled Susan into a sitting position and leaned her against the desk.

"If you want a sick note for court," said Erin "the doctor's leaving in a few minutes and so unfortunately, being in this state, you're going to miss him."

Susan's eyes immediately popped open. "Don't let the doctor go!" she said.

As Susan stood up, Erin grabbed her by the arm and propelled her through the exit door.

"And don't EVER come back and do that again on my shift!" she said.

Funnily enough, Susan never did come back to the department complaining of 'seizures' and the only other time that we saw her was when she was brought in by the police following a fight. She came in slowly and, with her eyes roaming the room said "That Irish one isn't here is she?"

Erin was a creature of habit and at one time we had a rest room where the night staff could take a quick nap during their break. Erin always had a sleep during her break, but had a habit of leaving her shoes outside the room when she was resting. One night Barry filled her shoes with ice from the department ice machine, and then pulled the emergency bell. Just to make sure, he banged on the rest room door and called for Erin. In no time at all Erin was up and shoving her feet into her shoes left outside the door. After a few moments of noisy shuffling of feet and loud swearing, we heard a thump – and silence. Erin had shoved her stockinged feet into her shoes, and then pulling them out just as quickly, had stood on a piece of ice, slipped and hit her head on the portable oxygen tanks kept outside the room.

Horrified, we got to her just as she was sitting up. Luckily there were no wounds on her head, although she did go home a bit early to recover.

When the morning staff came in for hand-over, we reported that Erin had to go home before the end of her shift as she had a 'nasty headache'. Funnily enough, nobody felt compelled to offer a fuller explanation.

≈ 25 ≈

Lost in Translation

In the summer months, due to the large influx of tourists, the population on our little island almost doubles. Some of the visitors are from beyond the UK and quite a few visit St Josephs at some time or other before returning home. The challenge of communicating with patients with very limited or non-existent English never gets any easier and when picking up the notes on an obviously foreign patient there is always a fervent hope that the patient can either understand or speak English, or has an adult with them to act as an interpreter. I say adult for a very good reason. Not all problems are a straight forward lacerated knee or twisted ankle and sometimes quite a detailed question and answer session is necessary to elicit a proper history.

An example of this is the Chinese lady who attended with her teenage daughter. Sometimes, we can call on a member of staff to translate as we have staff who can speak a myriad languages from Afrikaans to Polish, Tagalog (from the Philippines) to Hindi. However, generally it is a bit of 'pot luck' as to who happens to be on duty that day and unfortunately Chinese does not feature amongst the multi-cultural staff members. The lady patient attending with her daughter was complaining of abdominal pain and could neither speak nor understand English, but her daughter could communicate quite well and, as such, had come along to act as translator. A detailed question and answer session ensued about the patient's signs and symptoms and amongst these were questions about her bowel habits and menstrual cycle.

This is why a teenage daughter is not the best translator – no matter how close a relationship the mother and daughter have, it can get very awkward when discussing the frequency and consistency of your parents' bowel movements! After it was established that the patient had neither diarrhoea nor vomiting, I tried to find out if she was constipated at all. Obviously, the daughter had a bit more trouble explaining 'constipation' in Chinese and resorted to screwing up her face, miming a squatting action and grunting. Her mother was not constipated.

Continuing the 'twenty questions', I asked if she had eaten anything spicy or unusual recently. Bingo. The patient had been shopping yesterday and decided to buy some English candy – it appeared that the Chinese lady had bought some cherry flavoured Durex lube and, unable to read what it said on the bottle, had been eating it, thinking it to be a type of confectionary. After getting through about half a tube of the stuff, she began to suffer abdominal pain and feel ill. Luckily, the lube wasn't toxic and the patient suffered from no serious side effects. It was, however, quite awkward trying to explain, via her daughter, that what she had been eating was a lubricant designed for sexual enjoyment and not for oral consumption!

Of course, misunderstandings can happen at any time to anyone: such is human nature. Celine was a Senior House Officer who had come to work with us from her native France and although her English was perfect, she had a heavy French accent and coupling this with her slim figure and good looks meant that a lot of the male staff members found her very attractive. One of Celine's first patients at St Joseph's was Marilyn, a lady in her mid-seventies living in a nursing home. Marilyn had chronic breathing problems and came through regularly requiring nebulisers and, at times, antibiotics. This day's admission was much the same as any other. Marilyn had been having a bit more difficulty drawing breath than usual, and when she began coughing as well, the nursing home staff thought that a visit to A/E would be prudent. As Celine entered the cubicle in which Marilyn was resting, the old lady opened her eyes.

"Hello, I'm your doctor."

"No, you're not."

Confused, Celine started again.

"My name is Celine. I am the doctor looking after you. How can I help you?"

"No, you're not. You're far too young to be a doctor; my granddaughter's older than you. Get me a real doctor."

This had been a problem before, encountered both by Celine and Craig, a fellow Senior House Officer.

Craig was in his late twenties but looked like he should still be in short trousers. More than once patients had asked nervously if he was actually qualified, or if he was still a student. Craig had all manner of ways of dealing with this and usually tempered his answer to how the patient asked the question. Normally, he just stated patiently that he was twenty eight years old, had been a qualified doctor for a few years, and was fully experienced. End of story.

When a forty year old lorry driver came in with a nasty laceration to his forearm, Craig took a history from him and examined the cut. Returning a few minutes later to treat the injury, the patient said "Whoa, hang on there. Isn't the real doctor going to see me?"

Taking a deep breath, Craig tried to reassure the gentleman that he WAS a real doctor, and was in fact older than he looked. The patient wasn't quite sure whether to believe him or not, but in the end accepted treatment.

"So you've been doing this a while?" he said.

For some reason known only to him, Craig paused in the middle of suturing the man's forearm and said "Well no, I'm still at school but they've not sussed me out yet!"

The next twenty minutes were spent in damage control and the patient left muttering under his breath "Some people think they're soo funny!"

Returning to Celine's interaction with Marilyn, she was still having problems convincing Marilyn that she was old enough to be a real doctor, especially as her patient had it firmly fixed in her mind that Celine was a young college student. She kept telling her that she "should be on TV with those good looks." In the end, Celine resorted to calling one of the nursing staff into the cubicle to confirm that she really was a fully qualified doctor. Mollified, Marilyn consented to being examined.

Placing her stethoscope on the patient's chest, Celine asked her to breathe deeply in and out of her mouth for a few minutes. Slightly hard of hearing, Marilyn didn't appear to hear her.

"Mrs Edwards, big breaths, big breaths." repeated Celine.

With a sigh, Marilyn answered, "They used to be, my dear. Now they're just useless flaps of skin. I used to have a good handful just like yours!"

≈ 26 ≈

The Joy of Sex

This reminded me of when I was a second year student nurse working on a male medical ward. We had a delightful old gentleman who used to be a Navy Captain and had been admitted following a stroke. He had come from a residential home and was pleasantly confused, quite often thinking he was back on board his ship. The stroke had left him with limited mobility and a paralysed left arm and through the day whilst in bed he would slowly lean further and further to the left. Reaching an arm around him to help sit him upright one day, his right hand shot out and he firmly grabbed my left breast.

"Hey, you can't do that!" I said, removing his hand.

"Why not?" he said, "I like it!"

Not wanting to upset the patient, I told him that if I let him do that then I would have to let *everyone* do it, and not everyone was as pleasant as he was. That seemed to do the trick and although the patient never did it again, he earned the nickname 'the boob bloke in bed 5'.

As a young student nurse, I never really thought much about my elderly patients being people with sexual needs. In fact, no young person likes to think of their parents 'doing it', and here I was confronted by someone the same age as my grandfather thinking about 'it'. For some reason there comes a mythical, unspecified age in which a person is deemed 'old' and does innocuous things like watching 'Antiques Roadshow' on TV, or listening to 'The Archers' on Radio 4.

Mr Tibbet came in to A/E requesting specifically to see a male doctor. This was quite unusual. It was fairly common for a female patient with a 'personal problem' to request to see a female doctor, but rare for a male patient to request a doctor of the same sex. Mr Tibbet was an elderly gentleman and, booking in, reassured the receptionist that he had "nothing against the pretty young lady doctors but it was a man thing."

Roy, the senior doctor on duty, was more than happy to see Mr Tibbet, and was curious as to what the 'man thing' might be.

In the examining room, he set about asking what had brought Mr Tibbet into A/E.

"Love making," said Mr Tibbet.

Roy knew that if he gave him time, his patient would hopefully explain a little more fully, and a short while later he did.

"I've been a widower for nearly seven years now and I get lonely for intimate female company," he said. "My daughter suggested that I do an adult education course at the college."

Not quite sure where this was going, Roy stayed silent.

"It was about using computers for the first time, and that was how it all started," he said.

Now Roy *was* confused. He couldn't think of how Mr Tibbet could have wound up in A/E because of his college course. Eventually it transpired that the gentleman had met a lady on his course who was also widowed. They had decided to embark upon a relationship and, because he couldn't "do it the way he used to," they used their new found computer skills to order some Viagra on-line.

He had taken one tablet just before they retired to the bedroom, and finding that it didn't have any effect, took another five minutes later. He had now had an erection for some sixteen hours and was feeling very uncomfortable and rather worried.

Roy reassured his patient that his erection would eventually subside naturally but, having taken his blood pressure and pulse and finding both a bit high, advised him not to take any more, or in fact ANY medication not prescribed for him by a doctor.

'Love-making' problems are not confined to elderly patients, and in fact occur far more often in the younger generation. It was usual to have at least one female patient come into A/E each week with a foreign object in her vagina. These foreign objects ranged from fizzy drink bottles that became wedged when the patient 'fell' on them, to tampons that the patient had forgotten about, to condoms that fell off during the course of love making. Some nurses become quite good at removing these articles in the blink of an eye and Lauren, one of our Emergency Nurse Practitioners, was one of the most proficient 'fanny fishers' on the team!

Sacha was in her early twenties and had come in with something "stuck up there". She came into A/E alone one Friday lunchtime and said that the night before, the condom that her boyfriend had been wearing had come off whilst they were having sex.

"It happens a lot," she said. "He insists on getting ordinary condoms but one size DOES NOT fit all!"

This time, though, she could not get the offending condom out and was hoping that one of us could help her.

Whilst in the ENP room, Lauren asked if she had tried to remove it herself first.

"Of course I did!" she said. "I tried, and then Darren tried …. and I even stuck my fingers down my throat to see if I could vomit it up."

≈ 27 ≈

Even More Stuck Up

"Things stuck up there" are a regular occurrence and both men and women attend the department to have various 'foreign bodies' removed from places that they definitely should not have been placed. Most patients are a tad embarrassed and, occasionally a bit ashamed when they end up having to attend an Accident and Emergency department after an evening of stimulation, self or otherwise. Sometimes the patient comes alone and at other times, they are accompanied by a 'friend'. We have yet to see a patient accompanied by a parent – for obvious reasons (well, would *you* come into A/E with your mum and a presenting problem of 'electric toothbrush missing in rectum')?

Complaining of lower abdominal pain, a gentleman arrived in A/E alone. He was a very pleasant self-effacing man, if not a wee bit effeminate. Answering most questions with a smile, he was very co-operative and eventually, leaning over the edge of the trolley that he was on, he whispered conspiratorially; "something may have got wedged up there". The doctor examining him thought that he might be able to feel something as he pressed on the lower abdomen, but due to his patient's discomfort and the concern about what the problem might be, an abdominal x-ray was ordered.

Despite further questioning, the patient was a bit vague as to what, if anything, might be "wedged up there" and said that although this was a distinct possibility, he was quite sure that he hadn't placed anything in his rectum recently!

The x-ray came back, and looking at the screen, we could easily see the problem. Going back to the patient, the examining doctor said that it appeared that there were at least three candles quite a long way into the man's rectum.

"Ah, I remember now," he said, "We had a power cut a few days ago and I was putting candles around the house ready for when it got dark. I was in the middle of getting changed to go out and so I was walking around the house naked. Unfortunately, I slipped and fell on a candle and it must have got stuck up there."

The doctor reminded the patient that, in fact, he had got three candles "stuck up there", and after thinking for a moment or two, the patient responded "Yeah, that's right. I got up and then fell over again on the other one. And as soon as I got up that time, I tripped over the rug and fell on the third one."

He kept a totally straight face throughout his story telling, and I am still not sure to this day whether he really thought that we would believe him, or if he was expecting one of us to say "I don't think that's what happened at all!" and had a second story ready, just in case. As it was, the doctor kept an impassive face and just replied with "It's amazing what can happen when you walk around the house naked."

This was not the last time we saw that particular gentleman in the department. He came in a few months later complaining of bleeding from his back passage and had to be admitted for day surgery to repair a painful anal tear.

Danny and Jo came in together. They had been married for just six months and were still very much in love. They had been playing what Jo described as 'bedroom games', which involved racing each other across the bedroom, across the marital bed and back out into the hallway – nude.

Apparently, the winner of this 'race' got the dubious pleasure of inserting a can of hair mousse into the body of their partner. Why hair mousse, and why this was selected as a forfeit I really don't know – personally, I would rather a losing partner rustled up a yummy meal or even made me a cup of tea, but each to his own.

Anyway, it appeared that Danny was the fastest of the pair, as Jo had been the recipient of the bright red can of 'Shockwaves' hair mousse. They both attended the department together and were very concerned. Apparently, the forfeit had been paid and the can was no longer in situ.

However, the lid was.

It appeared that neither partner had thought to either check that the lid was tightly connected to the can, or had thought to remove it completely and it was firmly wedged high up in the vagina. Both partners had done their best to remove it, and in doing so had pushed it further in.

Without too much effort, Lauren managed to remove it using a pair of long nosed forceps and, embarrassed, the pair left none the worse for their 'game'.

≈ 28 ≈

Trust Me, I'm a Nurse!

After asking about foreign objects that other people insert into various orifices, the next question posed by acquaintances tends to be about an unusual lump, bump or rash that they've recently noticed. In social situations, I have been known to tell new acquaintances that I clean lavatories for a living to avoid people from giving me a blow by blow account of their groin rash or hairy underarm mole. It never ceases to amaze me how many relative strangers are prepared to regale me with tales of their dirty bathroom habits just because I am a nurse.

I have a friend who is a GP and he quite often suffers the same fate. In fact, he was once pulled aside at a family wedding, where a friend of the groom deftly dropped his trousers to show him a particularly nasty boil in the cleft of his buttocks!

Luckily, I have avoided *that* particular occurrence, although I have been on the receiving end of a story involving a particularly whiffy vaginal discharge whilst trying to enjoy a prawn and smoked salmon vol-au-vent at a party.

At the wake of the brother of a good friend, a bespectacled lady in her thirties sidled up to me.

"Is it true that you're a nurse?" she asked

Inwardly cursing whoever had told her, I agreed that I did *work* as a nurse, but, of course I was off duty at the moment. I was hoping that this might prevent the inevitable questions that follow, but nope, not a chance.

"I need to ask you something." she said. "It's a bit embarrassing though."

I told her that it was probably better that she saw her GP because he knew her medical history already and would probably be of more help.

"I'd rather speak to a woman," she said. "I've found a lump and I'm worried that I might have cancer."

"It really is best you see your own doctor," I told her. "He can examine both breasts and arrange for a mammogram or biopsy if necessary."

"No, my breasts are fine," she said. "The lump is *down there*." Of course it was. I should have figured that out as soon as she spoke to me – if someone doesn't want to see their GP and would prefer to tell their problems to a virtual stranger, then the problem is bound to be 'down there'.

I asked if she had spoken to anyone else about her problem, and it transpired that she was a single lady, living with and looking after her elderly mother, had no close female friends, and had never had a boyfriend.

I told her that I really couldn't advise on her lump without seeing it and I wasn't prepared to do that. Not particularly happy, but accepting my explanation, she went away and I thought that would be the last I heard of her. A few weeks later, I heard via my friend that this lady had actually heeded my advice and gone to her GP about her lump. It also transpired that this 'lump' was in fact her clitoris – and despite what she thought, she had had it for a lot longer than the few weeks that she thought it had been there.

It isn't only virtual strangers who ask for medical advice left, right and centre. Luckily my non-medical friends are kind enough to bypass me when needing medical advice and speak to their respective family doctors. Not so my mother-in-law.

Despite her disappointment at my 'being only a nurse' when I married her son (his last long term girlfriend had been a teacher, as were both my mother- and father-in-law), it didn't take her long to avail herself of my medical knowledge and it became a regular occurrence for her to start a telephone conversation with "I've got this pain……..".

After pointedly telling her, several times, that she needed to speak to her own doctor, she started frequenting her GP practice more often.

And then I began to get telephone calls beginning with "My doctor said I've got ……. Is that right?"!

I eventually resorted to saying that I would happily give her medical advice at any time – but would be charging her private patients' rates to do so. Following that, the phone calls became much less frequent, although they have yet to stop completely.

I suppose there are other occupations that can raise an eyebrow or two as well.

Early one morning a gentleman who worked in a funeral home called for an ambulance complaining of severe abdominal pains and nausea. He came into Accident and Emergency, where he was given some strong pain relief and tests were performed to determine the source of the pain.

The gentleman had come in with his wife and she spent her time brushing the hair off his forehead and gripping his hand tightly, whilst constantly reassuring him that she would "Look after him whatever the problem is." I could see that her attentiveness was irritating the patient in the next bed, but as her husband was obviously being kept distracted enough to stop him focusing on his pain, I did not interfere!

She told him that she had decided not to call in sick for him at work until we knew what was wrong, and she knew whether he would have to stay in hospital. When the results of the tests came back, it was as we suspected: the gentleman was suffering from kidney stones.

The lady turned to her husband and asked, "Would you like me to call the funeral home now?"

With a scornful look, one of the relatives of the patient in the cubicle next to him turned round and snapped, "Bloody hell, lady, he's not THAT sick!"

≈ 29 ≈

Check Up

Amazingly, some people would rather sit in a waiting room surrounded by sick and bleeding people instead of visiting their GP or local pharmacy. In my opinion, the five phrases no A/E nurse or doctor wants to hear are:

• "This is probably nothing, but I just want it checking out."

• "I've had this for ages, but I've got a day off today so thought I'd get it checked."

• "I've just come back from my GP and I want a second opinion."

• "My wife came in with chest pains and I thought, while she's here, I'd get this checked."

And finally, probably the worst of the bunch:

• "We're here on holiday and I didn't bother going to my local hospital because I usually have to wait ages."

Any of the above phrases can be guaranteed to raise the blood pressure and pulse rate of Accident and Emergency personnel and bring about murmured death threats, or at the very least, thoughts of doing actual bodily harm to those particular patients!

Although the phrase "I've come for a check-up," can make me shudder, sometimes the reason for the "check-up" can be quite amusing.

A young self-employed plumber in his twenties came in saying that he "thought he had E-Coli poisoning" and wanted us to "do a blood test" so that he could catch it early.

He had recently seen a television consumer programme about a person who had been seriously ill with this nasty infection and was sure that his slight stomach discomfort was caused by E-Coli.

Wanting to know exactly why and how the patient thought he had become infected I asked him if he could pin point any particular thing that he had eaten recently that made him feel unwell.

"Well," he said, "yesterday morning I had a job on the housing estate mending a leaking bathroom sink. I had my head under the bathroom sink with my basin wrench almost ready to make the repair when a little girl of about two years old tapped me on my leg and handed me the cup of 'tea' she had brought me. She had this miniature tea set that she was sitting in the hallway playing with. I smiled at her and drank down the tea, which was really just water, and handed her the small cup back. Before I could reposition myself under the sink she tapped me on my leg again with more 'tea'. I didn't want to upset her and as her mum was across the hall in her bedroom doing something, I didn't want to call her to take her daughter away because she was a really nice kid.

"Anyway" he continued "I tossed this one down as well and then I realized she was too small, this was happening way too fast for her to have gone downstairs, and she couldn't reach the kitchen sink anyway. As I watched her I was shocked to see she was dipping the little cup into the toilet. That was my tea."

I said to him that he would probably be fine as, although lavatory water wasn't exactly sterile, it shouldn't do him any harm.

"Unless," I said, smiling, "it had been well used and not flushed."

The poor man's face said it all: it appeared that, indeed, it had been "well used and not flushed"!

Small patients, usually those under the age of five, can be quite logical and, if asked in the right way, can give quite a sensible account of their presenting problem. I do emphasise, though, the need to ask the right questions!

A three year old girl told her mummy that she had put a bright, shiny bead up her nose. Her mum looked and couldn't find it and so practically threw the poor child into the car and drove her to the hospital.

Unfortunately, it also happened to be a bank holiday Monday and so the department was full of other patients and both mum and her daughter had quite a long wait.

No problem for Daisy as she was happily playing in the toy room, although her mother was getting more anxious by the hour. Eventually, they were called into the department where, with minimal prompting, Daisy confirmed that, yes, she had indeed put a bead up her nose, and helpfully even recalled which nostril that the bead had gone up.

The young and fairly new doctor on duty checked both nostrils and, not finding any foreign body, decided to x-ray Daisy's face in order to determine the position of the offending bead.

Although her mum was really quite worried, Daisy was remarkably calm and accepted being poked, prodded and x-rayed without any fuss – until mum asked if Daisy would need an operation to remove the bead. At that, the poor child burst into tears and said that she didn't *want* to have an operation and anyway, everyone was asking if she had put the bead *up* her nose but no-one had asked her if she had got it down again!

Apparently, almost as soon as the bead had been placed in her nose, it had been sneezed out again, however, as Daisy quite rightly pointed out, no-one had actually thought to ask her if it was still in there!

Sometimes it's asking the right questions. And other times it's using the right words.

I grew up in a household of two sisters and four brothers and as second oldest, I become fairly proficient at changing a baby's nappy. For some reason, my brothers' private parts were known as their 'front tail', whilst us girls had a 'front bit'. These phrases must have originated from my mother and I remember being quite shocked when I got a bit older and realised that the penis had more than one name, and 'front tail' was not one of them!

Entering the world of medicine, I was (and still am) surprised at the variation of names for both male and female parts of the anatomy. The vagina has quite a few nicknames, some more well-known than others, while there are many, many more nicknames for the penis and/or testicles.

Needless to say, lots of patients of both genders attend the Accident and Emergency department and spend a while shuffling their feet and looking down at the floor with burning cheeks before stating that their problem is their 'willie' or 'fanny'. A lot of these patients are of the younger generation, as older people tend to be a bit more forthright and a little less embarrassed regarding body parts and bodily functions.

A young man in his twenties booked into reception, along with a much older gentleman of seventy or so. Picking up Henry's card, I glanced at his name and called him through to the triage room. Walking into the room slowly, he stood just inside the open doorway, where he paused.

"Come on in." I said, "What is the problem?"

Staying in the doorway, the young man said "Well it's not *my* problem as such, it's my old man. My dad said to come here."

"Ok," I said "Where is he? Is he on his way in?"

"Who?" asked the patient.

Feeling as if one of us was not quite making sense, I repeated "Your old man. Where is he?"

"Oh, my old man's here," said Henry, and in one swift movement he shut the door and dropped his jeans, exposing everything from navel to knees. He was not wearing any underwear.

"My foreskin is really tight," he said, waving his penis in my general direction. "It's cutting the circulation off to my old man and my dad said I might need a circumvention!"

At the beginning of the eighties, while still a student nurse, one of my earliest– and most enjoyable – placements was on the children's ward. Although some quite sick children are patients on these wards, the paediatric units in hospitals are bright and cheerful. The nurses wear bright tabards adorned with cartoon characters and the walls have the likes of Winnie-the-Pooh, Paddington Bear and Sponge Bob Square Pants parading across them. One of the most important things that we were taught when beginning our time on paediatrics was to find out three things: the name of the child's favourite toy, the name(s) of their pet(s), and the names of any siblings. By the time that I had finished my three month placement, a fourth item had been added to the list – how a smaller child asked to use the toilet.

This all came about after a lovely little boy came into the children's ward for the usual five day stay associated with a tonsillectomy. These days, a tonsillectomy is performed as a day procedure, but in the early eighties it entailed a five day stay, and parents could only visit for two hours in the afternoon. Consequently children spent much more time in the company of the nursing staff and we were a lot more involved in their daily routine than happens now.

Little Darren was a gorgeous child with big blue eyes and a blonde 'basin style' haircut. He came into the ward a bubbly, happy child and his planned tonsillectomy went without a hitch. However, the day following his operation, he began crying for his grandmother and wetting his bed regularly. Often, one of the nurses would sit and hold him whilst he sobbed "I want to visit Grandma." She would explain that he would see Grandma soon, and maybe she would visit that afternoon or the next.

"But I want to visit Grandma NOW." he would sob.

After two days, and seeing only his mother visiting, one of the nurses pulled his mum to one side just as she was leaving and stated that we were a bit concerned about little Darren, he was quite withdrawn most of the time, had been wetting his bed regularly, and spent a lot of time crying for his grandmother. She asked if his grandmother would be visiting, so that we could at least reassure Darren that he would be seeing grandma soon.

"Oh no," said mum "Grandma's been bed bound since her stroke several years ago. She has a downstairs bedroom in what used to be the dining room, between the lounge and the downstairs toilet."

Expecting that Darren must be missing seeing his grandma, the same nurse said that must be what Darren meant – he must be missing going into her bedroom to visit.

"No, Darren doesn't see her much," his mum explained. "She's usually asleep with the door closed."

Confused, the nurse then asked if his mum had any idea why Darren spent so much time crying that he needed to visit Grandma, when he hardly ever saw her when he was home.

"Well, he doesn't really mean he wants to *visit Grandma*," she said. "He means that he wants to go to the toilet. It's a sort of code that we've invented. It happened because Grandma's bedroom is next to the toilet and Darren is shy about asking to go to the toilet if we have company. We've decided that if Darren asks to visit Grandma, then only I will know that he needs to go to the toilet and the people around us will be none the wiser."

No, and neither will the nurses trying to look after the poor child in his mother's absence.

We all felt incredibly guilty after this, for not somehow figuring out that this was what Darren had meant and putting two and two together regarding his bed wetting episodes.

It did all turn out well in the end. Almost immediately Darren stopped wetting the bed, got taken to the toilet promptly every time he asked to "visit Grandma" and had heaps of forbidden treats given to him to help assuage the guilt of the nursing staff!

≈ 30 ≈

A Well Earned Rest

The busiest time in the Accident and Emergency department just happens to be the time at which a lot of the staff want to have their own family holidays. The nursing staff is restricted to just one week off as annual leave during July and August, and two weeks over Easter.

The fairest way of arranging the holidays was for each person to request the time off that they particularly wanted and then liaise amongst themselves if too many people wanted the same weeks off. Generally this system worked quite well and in April 2010 myself, my husband and our teenage son went to India for two weeks.

A good time was had by all, and while away I kept in contact with my colleagues back home, secretly gloating when I heard how busy it was in the department. Jokingly, I told various members of staff that I was having such a good time that I just might not return.

Really, you'd think I'd have learned to keep my mouth shut by now, for – totally coincidentally – in Iceland the Eyjafjallajokull volcano was erupting. This Icelandic volcano 'woke up' on 14th April and a heavy ash cloud closed the air space over many countries. We happened to be booked to fly home to Gatwick Airport on 15th April, just as all airlines from India, and indeed nineteen other countries, grounded their 'planes.

In a way, I was glad that it was such a large and well publicised eruption, as I was almost certain that otherwise I would not have been believed, and it would have been presumed that I was 'pulling a sickie'. (Contrary to popular opinion, during my entire time at St Joseph's I never once called in sick when I wasn't ill!)

As it was, within half a day of the news of the eruption, and subsequent delays to travellers, a memo was issued by the NHS Trust stating that any member of staff that had extra days off due to the ash cloud, would have to 'pay back' the extra time taken off.

Luckily, while stuck in New Delhi and unable to get a flight home, I was not aware of this unsympathetic dictum from my employers and so I did not have that worry to cope with as well. Having had a really good holiday and just about reached the end of our budget we were ready to return home.

Not sure now of how long we would be out of the country, I contacted the department and let them know the situation. Meanwhile, our son was going stir-crazy as we had been instructed to stay in the hotel in case the airline contacted us with an available flight.

We stayed there for the next six days. We were glad that the hotel had a swimming pool as April 2010 also just happened to be the hottest April in Delhi for over fifty years!

We paid for our room and food on a day by day basis with a credit card, and kept our fingers crossed that a flight home would come through before it 'maxed out'. Each morning we phoned the airline only to be told that there were still no flights.

We were glad that we had actually *had* our holiday and were waiting to return, as the news was full of travellers stuck at their departing airports, sleeping on the floors and not able to fly to their chosen destinations. Had that been our situation, not only would we have lost our holiday, but I wouldn't have been able to take any other time off until the following year.

Many people come to our little island on holiday and find that one of the first things they end up doing is coming into A/E to get a prescription for their medication because they've left theirs at home. Or they underestimate the amount that they need and run out before the end of their holiday, and have to come to see us. The people who cannot organise their medication needs end up wasting a day of their holiday, as well as taking up the time of the hospital and doctors who have to write prescriptions for the medication.

Every time that I go on holiday myself, I carefully count out my medication and ensure that I have enough for the full time that I am there. As usual, on this holiday, I took enough to cover the full two weeks and an extra couple of days 'just in case'. Unfortunately, I didn't take enough medication to allow for an extra week of volcanic activity in Iceland. Hence, one of *our* 'extra' days was spent going to the local hospital. After waiting for a few hours to see a doctor, he gave me a prescription for the hospital pharmacy – which stocked only analgesics and antacids! The pharmacist was very helpful and told me that I could "try some of the local chemists".

Our next step was hiring a local tuk-tuk and driver and trawling around all of the pharmacies within a twenty mile radius. Luckily the tuk-tuk driver seemed to know where most of these were situated and at each establishment, the pharmacist reached below the counter to a large unlabelled container containing hundreds of blister packs of various medications, and telling us to "take out what you need."

These containers were holding everything from 10mg Diazepam tablets to almost pure Codeine to Prozac – and much more in between. It was an addicts dream!

Eventually I managed to find one drug, albeit by a different manufacturing company, and had to forgo the second one altogether. I did, however, complete my time in India without being ill, so *something* worked!

A week later, airspace around the world reopened and we were finally able to get a flight home.

I got back into work a week later than I was originally meant to and was met by my manager informing me that I "owed the department several days" or I could take the extra time that I had been away as unpaid leave and they would dock my pay accordingly. In contrast, when my husband returned to *his* work with the local council, he was asked if the family was okay and reassured that as the extra time off was enforced and of no fault of his own, he would not be penalised.

It's good to work in a caring profession!

≈ 31 ≈

Appropriate Attendance

Sometimes, I quite strongly believe that – great as the National Health Service is – our work would be a lot easier if certain members of the general public had to pay for some of their treatment. It certainly would reduce the amount of drunk patients attending the department and taking up a bed, and intravenous fluids, whilst they sober up. I have lost count of how many times a person has called an ambulance because their friend/relative/neighbour has drunk too much alcohol and cannot stand up, or is vomiting. If a charge for treatment of this sort of 'complaint' was introduced I am sure that concerned relatives would think it was just fine to let Uncle Bill sober up on the couch.

One weekend a lady came in who had had a Caesarean section eleven days previously and, booking herself in, she said that she had attended in order to get her staples taken out. I was a bit non-plussed as to why she had attended A/E rather than having the midwife or her own doctor remove them. She had been discharged from the maternity unit just a couple of days earlier and had been told that when she had her staples removed, she and her baby would also be checked thoroughly. Obviously, as we didn't know her or her baby, and hadn't seen her at any time during her pregnancy, she wouldn't be getting any sort of continuity of care seeing a different doctor in A/E.

The lady attended with her husband and two young children, plus had her new-born baby in tow.

As soon as I called her into the triage room, I told her that she should go to her own doctor or midwife.

"I should have been seen by her yesterday, but the sales were on and I went shopping instead, so I came here today for you to do it," she said!

I told her quite firmly that she should see the person that she was supposed to have seen the day before because, after all, she had had major surgery and needed checking out fully.

Whilst in the triage room (with the rest of her young children, who were in the process of opening various cupboards, and sliding on and off the large examining chair) she began pouting like a five year old child.

"You mean you won't just take my staples out?" she asked.

"You have to go to your own doctor or midwife," I said. "That's why you had an appointment in the first place."

"I can't believe you made me wait here for ages to tell me that!" exclaimed the patient. "That's what you're here for. I don't believe this. I'm making a complaint!"

She had been waiting in the waiting room for all of ten minutes before being called into the triage room. With that, she gathered up her children, and bemused husband – who had neither moved nor spoken since he sat down on the chair next to her – and stormed out. A complaint never did materialise, about which I was quite sorry, as a reply might have helped go some little way to educating her about 'appropriate attendance'.

Appropriate attendance is the one thing that *some* of the general public really need educating about, and there is the occasional advertising campaign poster seen around the place with a list of appropriate problems with which to attend A/E (bearing in mind that A/E does actually stand for ACCIDENT and EMERGENCY)!

Within the very same week that the lady requiring her C-section staple removal came in, a mother and father attended with their two-year old child. He had a runny nose, mild cough, congestion and intermittent fever. Basically, a cold. I really try not to be impatient with parents because generally they are doing the best they can, and I know from my own parental experience that it's hard taking responsibility for another human being, especially a really little one. But in my head I was thinking "really? Do you *really* think this needs to be seen in Accident and Emergency at 8pm?"

I was then even more irritated because about two minutes after meeting this family, I discovered that they had already been to their own GP a day and a half earlier (almost exactly 36 hours). Their doctor had prescribed antibiotics for the child less than two days ago. So they were seen, examined, evaluated and treated. But that had been a full 36 hours ago and the child was not completely well yet!

The parents were insisting that the A/E doctor give their little darling "something else" because the medicine given by their GP obviously "hadn't worked". Despite being told that they should return to their GP, the mother point blank refused and said that she "knew her rights" and knew that, by law, we couldn't turn her away or refuse to see her child.

I filled in a set of notes for the child and handed it to one of the casualty officers to see him.

On examination (punctuated by instructions by the mother to 'check his ears' and 'make sure that his glands are alright') it was established that the child had a cold, plain and simple. And colds are viruses. Viruses are not bacteria, so the antibiotic that he had been given wasn't going to make him better anyway.

Having met the parents, I came to the conclusion that their GP undoubtedly put the child on antibiotics as the path of least resistance. Many patients do not believe a doctor who says that antibiotics (or x-rays, or CT, or blood tests, etc.) are not indicated, and obviously the GP didn't have the time, effort, or energy, to argue the point with these parents.

He was discharged nearly four hours later with the advice to encourage fluid intake, and that he would get better without any extra help. By this time, the child was also exceedingly tired and grumpy and would have been better served by being tucked up in his own bed for the last few hours.

On the other hand, there are times when people attend A/E with great reluctance although they really need to be seen. Often these patients are elderly people who still have a great respect for doctors and don't want to 'waste anyone's time'. It is almost guaranteed that these patients have a genuine illness or injury and have suffered for hours, and sometimes days, because they feel that someone else is more deserving of the hospital's time.

One afternoon an elderly widow came in by ambulance with a badly injured ankle. She was a delightful lady in her late seventies who had lived alone with just her tabby cat for company since losing her husband several years earlier. On her way into the kitchen, the cat had wound itself between her feet and she had tripped over him, landing with her right foot underneath her. This caused a fracture to her right ankle, but rather than press the emergency button that she wore around her neck, she struggled to her feet to use the telephone as she 'didn't want to disturb anyone'. From the telephone in the hallway, she rang her daughter to say that she had fallen. After questioning by her daughter, she admitted that her foot was a "bit sore" but told her daughter to collect the children from school and to give them their tea before she came round to see her.

Child duties done, the daughter then went round to check her mother's 'sore foot' only to find that the fracture was now a displaced fracture dislocation, caused when the lady had stood up and limped to the phone. Her daughter had taken one look at the strangely angled foot, which was badly discoloured, and, despite the lady's protestations, called an ambulance. On arrival at A/E, the lady was very apologetic for taking up the time of all of the staff that attended to her and stated that she'd have stayed at home, but it was "starting to smart a bit". She said that she was sure that there were other people in the department more deserving of our time.

This lovely lady ended up needing emergency surgery in order to save her foot, and if she had left it for very much longer before attending, would have lost the foot altogether. These are the patients that make you feel really quite humble, and remind you of why you do the job in the first place.

Other patients have their own reasons for not attending hospital when they really should do so.

David, a thirty year old chef in a pub had had an accident a week ago and burned his left hand with hot fat. Phoning his wife from work, she advised him to put butter on the burn and bandage it up. Returning home, it was still really painful, so he washed the butter off (I didn't think that this old wives' tale still existed!), put another bandage on it and took a couple of painkillers. After a week of treating it this way, it had got no better and so, reluctantly, he came in to see us. Unwinding the smelly bandage, I was confronted with a green, infected wound and discoloured tissue. How this gentleman had put up with the incredible pain, I really don't know, but it must have been excruciating.

After being seen by the casualty officer, the patient was referred for surgery and ended up losing part of his hand. He had not attended with the original injury as it was "an occupational hazard" and he didn't want to take a few hours out of work on a busy Saturday.

≈ 32 ≈

What's in a Name?

In order for a patient to go from the waiting room to either the triage room, or into the department proper, one of the members of staff has to physically go into the waiting room and call them. This is not always as easy as it sounds, and more than once, I've taken one look at a patients name and thought "I can't pronounce that!". More often than not, they are names of foreign extraction, although there are some difficult to pronounce Cornish names out there too. If I cannot find another member of staff to show me how to pronounce it (or even better, call the patient in for me), then I use the 'presenting complaint' to give me a heads up and will quietly approach the person who I think might be the patient and say "Are you Mr Alojzy Czeslaw? I apologise if I've pronounced your name wrong."

Easy enough if the patient has a hand injury and Mr Czeslaw is the only man in the waiting room with a hand injury, harder if it becomes multiple choice!

Foreign names are hard; amusing names are even worse. What on earth were Mr and Mrs Willie thinking when they named their daughter Henrietta, or Mr and Mrs Udder, when they called their daughter Anne? There are times that a set of notes has been handed to two or three different people, because no-one wants to stand at the entrance to the waiting room and call "Mrs Fartwell!"

Some names are the human equivalents of the tautonyms encountered in the world of zoology, where the genus and species names are identical, as with *Ratus ratus* and *Gorilla gorilla.*

This is reasonably easy to deal with if you read the name carefully before just calling in the patient. Calling "Mr Dick" is a lot simpler if you look first, instead of standing there like a lemon calling for "Dick Dick"!

I really can't say that this is something that occurred to me when I first started to work in the department, but, despite being aware that there are some hilarious names out there, it's easy to get into a rhythm of calling in patients by both names without thinking. Using both first and surnames prevents two, or even three, patients all getting up at once when you call in "Mrs Jones" or "Mr Smith".

Paige Turner, or Gladys Friday are easy to call in as Miss Turner or Mrs Friday, but sometimes easy avoidance isn't possible.

Mr Cockfit could not be called anything other than that because with a waiting room full of people – a lot of whom were male – just looking for a patient with a presenting complaint of 'painful big toe' and with the first name of Peter doesn't help. At these times you just have to bite the bullet and try to persuade other staff members to do your dirty work for you. This is where student nurses can be indispensable.

Some members of staff, of course decide to make life difficult for themselves with absolutely no assistance, and Denise really didn't help herself by standing at the entrance to the waiting room and, mispronouncing Hugh's name, called in Mr HUGE Raleef.

Most of us, at some point, have had our own faux pas with patients. These are easy mistakes to make as we are all seeing lots of patients, all of whom are new to us, and sometimes we make assumptions about patients and the people accompanying them. One thing that I now do, after putting my large foot in it more than once, is to check the relationship of the friend/relative accompanying the patient *before* opening my mouth.

More than once, I have begun a conversation with "did your mum bring you in today?" to be told "no, this is my wife", or, to a couple holding hands, "and you are her partner?" only to be told curtly "No, I'm her brother."

An excusable mistake occurred when the patient with long blonde hair and sapphire blue eyeshadow arrived. The patient had been brought in semi-conscious and was helped from a car onto a trolley.

Unable to get any sense from the patient, I asked the gentleman with her "What has happened to her tonight?"

The friend replied "HE has been drinking. He is pre-op at the minute. *Pre-op* darling. 'She' is still a HE. Kevin is hardly a female name, now, is it?"

Kicking myself for not looking at the patient's name on their notes, I made a mental note to at least get the gender right in future, even if not the relationship.

Some people, however, seem to go out of their way to explain their relationship to each other to you.

A lady in her fifties came in with her friend. As I called them into the triage room, I said "hello" to Ms Lancaster and followed it up with "and are you Ms Lancaster's friend?" Mistake.

"No," she said "We are lesbian partners. We've been living together as partners for over thirty years. In the days when we first met, people were really prejudiced and so when we bought our first house together we said we were just friends. We've moved house since then and now we live near to my brother. None of our families understand about lesbians and what a loving relationship gay people can have. Our families still think that we are just friends but first and foremost we are a lesbian couple in love and it is a beautiful relationship."

Okay, really that was more information than I needed, especially when it transpired that Ms Lancaster had attended because she caught her finger in her car door that morning and was worried that it might be broken!

The worst of these mistakes, however, was when an elderly lady – many years post menopause – came in complaining of abdominal pain and bleeding from "down below". I took a history from her as I took her blood pressure and then said that I needed her to get undressed.

"Would you like your friend to stay whilst you get changed, or would you prefer him to wait outside?" I asked

"I don't really mind too much," she said, "but we don't know each other, the nurse sent him in."

It appeared that when placing the patient in the cubicle, I had forgotten to write her name on the whiteboard in the department, and from glancing at the board, the cubicle still appeared to be empty. Hence, one of the other nurses had directed the next patient to the cubicle and told him to just "Take a seat in there, I'll be in in a minute."

The elderly gentleman had done just that, and neither patient had thought to put their head out of the closed curtain to say that there was already a patient in there!

≈ *33* ≈

Scrambled Egg

Generally, after a few years 'on the job', there are very few things that gross healthcare staff out – cleaning up a pool of vomit just before tucking into your lunchtime sandwich or discussing that morning's doubly incontinent patient whilst eating supper is just run of the mill stuff. Sometimes, though, something can put you off a foodstuff for life.

Once upon a time, I enjoyed eating scrambled egg; after having Mrs Lyons as a patient, I went off it for ever!

Mrs Lyons came into the department by ambulance from the nursing home in which she resided. As she came through the door, I noticed that the paramedic accompanying her was almost nose to nose with her and shouting "WE'RE AT THE HOSPITAL NOW."

It transpired that Mrs Lyons was very hard of hearing and a little bit confused to boot. She was wearing a loose tent-style dress and as she was transferred from the ambulance trolley to the Accident and Emergency department trolley, a large glob of scrambled egg rolled out from beneath a fold of fabric. Aaron, the paramedic, explained that Mrs Lyons had just finished eating her lunch as they collected her, and the main component seemed to have been scrambled egg. The crew had waited for their patient to finish her lunch before bringing her to hospital.

As the golf ball sized lump of scrambled egg rolled out from within the depths of her dress, quick as a flash, her hand shot out, deftly picked up the lump and stuffed it into her mouth.

I began to explain to Mrs Lyons that we would have to help her out of her clothes and into a hospital gown, and would then run a few simple clinical tests. The patient just looked straight past me and continued to chew on her lump of scrambled egg (she was minus her dentures and so was steadily gumming it to death). Remembering that she was hard of hearing, I leaned forward and began speaking in a louder voice, a few inches away from her face.

At exactly the same time as I leaned forward and upped the volume, the patient began making slight gurgling noises in her throat. She screwed up her face, closed her eyes tight – and then a large ball of scrambled egg erupted from her mouth.

In slow motion, the ball of semi chewed, partly sucked scrambled egg came flying at me, trailing bits and pieces of spittle in its wake.

My brain was working overtime, shouting at me to move out of the way, but the body was not co-operating. Time sped up and the ball of soggy scrambled egg slammed into my face. Involuntarily, I inhaled sharply and in doing so, small bits of scrambled egg entered my mouth.

Generally, I am pretty resilient and can cope with most things thrown up on me, spilt on me or thrown at me. This, however, beat everything else into a cocked hat. I felt my stomach begin to churn, and stepped back from the trolley heaving. I was desperately trying not to throw up my recently eaten lunch, and had tears rolling down my face as I heaved. I could feel the slimy pieces of scrambled egg in my mouth and my mind kept shouting "That came out of an old lady's mouth!" This really did not help, and Aaron was of no assistance as he was giggling like a schoolgirl.

I disappeared off into the staff room and rinsed my mouth out over and over with water. Really, I wanted to use neat disinfectant, or even better, pure ethanol, but neither were practical or possible.

I went back into the department, to find Mrs Lyons still sucking on stray bits of scrambled egg oblivious to the near loss of my lunch, and the paramedics still snorting with laughter at my misfortune.

I still cannot bear the taste or texture of scrambled egg, and in fact just looking at the stuff makes my stomach do back flips. It will probably take many more years, a large amount of therapy and a degree of Alzheimer's to make me ever again eat eggs that have been scrambled.

≈ 34 ≈

TV Trauma

Over the years, many patients have stated that it "must be nice to work in a real life 'Holby City' ,"or "it must be just like being on 'Casualty' working here," although in real life, patients are rarely as quickly and easily treated as they are on TV dramas, and *very* rarely are the doctors George Clooney look-a-likes! TV dramas see patients examined, tested, x-rayed, referred to speciality services, discharged on to wards and seen by their consultant all within an hour of admission. A wonderful idea, but the stuff of fiction. There is also a lot less in the way of personal relationships within the department. In the real world, there is a distinct lack of nurses and doctors sneaking off into offices and store rooms for a quick fling together! Public perception can be quite amusing though, and I did have a patient not long ago who, along with his brother, were obviously devotees of hospital dramas.

David had come into the department on Sunday morning feeling unwell. Unsurprisingly for a lad in his twenties, he had been out drinking the night before. He was adamant that he was not hungover as he had 'only drunk seven or eight pints,' and was backed up by his brother who insisted that this was a great deal less than he normally drank. David was complaining of feeling sick and dizzy and was sure that his drink had been 'spiked' the night before. He had recently watched a hospital drama on TV and there was a patient there who had attended an emergency department seriously ill after having his drink 'spiked' with narcotics. David was sure that this was what had happened to him because he had left his drink unattended whilst he went to the toilet and there were several people standing around the bar area where his drink was sitting. He was insisting that we treat him for a narcotics overdose before he 'collapses and nearly dies like the bloke on Casualty'.

It took quite a while to convince him that his life was not in danger and if he was going to be seriously ill from an overdose the night before, it would be obvious by now.

TV dramas have a lot to answer for!

A similar episode occurred a short while later, but with far more serious results. The paramedics had been called to an address where a young man had collapsed. Bringing him into the resuscitation room, it was obvious that the young man was in a bad way. He was barely conscious and breathing very shallowly, and was accompanied by a friend who, although conscious, was bleary eyed and slurring his speech.

Apparently, these two geniuses had seen a TV programme where two men had appeared to take a cocktail of illicit substances and had been full of energy that night – dancing the evening away and then having a prolonged orgy with several pretty young ladies. Thinking that that was a good idea, they had embarked upon mixing some pills that they bought from another friend with their copious amounts of beer. Not surprisingly, the younger of the two men had become quite ill rather quickly.

Unable to get any response from the patient, and needing information, I asked the friend what had happened.

"Well, the thing is," he started, "One minute he was talking about going to see Arsenal play next weekend, and the next minute he was, like, not answering my questions."

This was all said in slow motion, with the words being drawn out and barely recognisable through the man's slurred speech.

Trying to get an idea of what they might have taken and how long ago, I asked the friend if he had brought any of the pills with him. I had to interrupt him several times with the same question as he had worked himself up into a state, rambling on about the fact that the patient had offered to take him to watch his beloved Arsenal play. "He can't take me if he's dead, can he?" he continued "And I was gonna get in free and everything!"

Asking again if he knew what the 'pills' were, the friend looked at me as if I had got two heads.

"Look," he said "can't you just give him some of that stuff that they give in Holby?"

Taking a deep breath, I stated firmly that Holby City was make-believe and just a story written for TV, and this was real life and his friend's life could really be in danger.

He stamped his foot impatiently and said that he *knew* all of that, but that he also knew that the TV dramas used the names of 'real drugs' to make the show that much more realistic.

"So I know what will wake him up," he said, "he needs some of that stuff you put in a needle."

Not really wanting to know, but knowing he was going to tell me anyway, I asked what 'stuff' he was talking about.

"You know," he said, "that drug they always use – he needs some Stat!"

≈ 35 ≈

Have *You* had an Accident?

Unfortunately, rather like the United States, Britain is becoming more and more of a 'compensation culture'. Whereas a few years ago, if a person tripped over a slightly raised paving slab, or leaned against a fence that collapsed, resulting in a scratched arm, they would treat their minor injury at home and probably laugh about it to their friends the next day, perhaps just feeling a little bit silly about their clumsiness. Not now, not with the amount of TV and radio airtime taken up by the multitude of law firms eager to help you to sue anyone and everyone if you have had an accident that is deemed not to be of your own making.

Since the advent of these advertisements, the amount of people attending Accident and Emergency Departments with very minor injuries caused by a trip, fall, or minor fender bender, has increased substantially. Patients are now attending Casualty departments all over the country having "nearly broken my ankle" or "almost dislocated my shoulder" resulting from not watching where they were going. The most common of all, though, has to be the "neck pain" caused by a whiplash injury to an occupant of a vehicle involved in a shunt. Road Traffic Incidents, as they are officially known, are a regular occurrence, and true whiplash is a painful sprain to the neck muscles that can take quite a while to heal. It is also quite difficult to prove as there is no bruising or swelling to see, and the diagnosis is made partly on the history of the incident.

Some people are experts at suffering from 'whiplash' and know exactly where the 'pain' is and exactly how it occurred. Most of the time, though, these patients have had a minor bump in their car and see the opportunity to lever some cash out of the insurance company.

Andrew came into Accident and Emergency via ambulance, complaining that he had "really bad whiplash" after he had had to brake sharply to avoid an animal in the road and a lady driving behind him had driven into the back of his red Mazda MX5 sports car. The patient had called the ambulance himself and, on its arrival, had insisted that the paramedics convey him to hospital to "see a doctor". Although they were not too concerned about his injury, the paramedics brought him into the casualty department due to his complaint of a painful neck injury (although they reported that when they arrived at the scene, the patient was pacing up and down moving his head from side to side and shouting at the tearful lady driver that had collided with his car).

While I was taking a history from the paramedic that had delivered Andrew to the department, the patient kept interjecting with his own remarks. When I asked the speed that he thought that the other driver was going at the time of impact, he could only recall that she must have been going "way too fast", even though the paramedic stated that neither car was damaged: there was just a little bit of white paint from the lady's Nissan Micra on the back of his Mazda. Still, Andrew insisted that he had been thrown forward in his seat and then back again from the force of the impact. This, he said, was what had caused the excruciating pain on the right side of his neck. The paramedic looked down at his notes, and then back up at the patient.

"I thought that the pain was on the left side of your neck?" he said. "That was what you told me when I attended you at the roadside."

Looking non-plussed for a minute, Andrew stated that the left side of his neck *did* hurt, but since being taken to hospital the right side of his neck hurt more than the left.

Leaving the patient with us, the paramedic went back to his ambulance and I continued to take the history. Andrew gave me a full, blow by blow account of the "speeding" lady driver that had "slammed into his car" and who had probably caused a "life changing injury" to his neck. He was quite lucky, he told me, to have come out of it alive! He wanted to make sure that I wrote down everything that he said and paused several times to ensure that I had got the facts right. A little later, I left him alone in the cubicle to await the doctor, and as I left I heard him make a phone call to his girlfriend to "write down that phone number for the injury lawyer people off the telly".

The doctor arrived to examine him a while later and found him sitting on the edge of the trolley eating a bar of chocolate and swinging his legs back and forth in boredom. After checking for any other injury, the doctor then asked him about the pain in his neck. It was, said Andrew, the worst pain that he had had in his life. It was causing him to have a blinding headache and made him feel quite sick.

Examining the left side of his neck, the patient began screwing up his face and mewling with pain. He stated that it was far too painful to touch. Moving to check the back of his neck, the pain was tolerable, but when the right side of his neck was examined, Andrew stated "that bit was ok". Double checking, he was asked again where the pain was and he insisted that the pain was on the left side and was "now moving round towards the back as well". Reminding him that he had first stated that this pain had started on the left side of his neck, before migrating to the right side and then back again to the left, Andrew thought about it for a while and then said that the pain was so all encompassing that he didn't know *where* it started and ended!

Needless to say, Andrew did not get his requested doctors report citing a serious neck injury, and was most disgruntled to be discharged with advice to take simple anti-inflammatory pain killers if the pain should not improve within a day or so.

Most patients with injuries caused by road traffic incidents are visited by the police, either for a statement, or a breath test for alcohol if they were the driver of a vehicle. Usually this occurs when the patient is still in the Accident and Emergency department, and if the patient has only minor injuries, it can save a lot of time and effort on following up an incident both for the driver and the police force.

The taking of a brief statement by the police can sometimes elicit quite humorous responses from the motorist who is insistent that the minor accident was anyone's fault but theirs. I suppose that both police and insurance companies are quite used to hearing a wide variety of reasons and excuses for an accident, but I never fail to chuckle at the motorists who "accidently hit the car in front because it was stationary" or who "swerved to avoid the tree that wasn't there earlier that morning", or, my personal favourite, "The accident happened, officer, because I was busy waving to the woman whose car I hit last week and therefore I hadn't noticed that the traffic in front of me had stopped!"

Mr Johnson was a patient who was involved in a single car collision – his 4 month old silver Mercedes c180 Kompressor had collided with a large and unyielding oak tree on a country road that afternoon. Mr Johnson had been driving along on the unseasonably warm day with his sun roof open and his favourite music on the radio when, in his words, "some yob had thrown a stone through the sunroof of the car, nearly knocking me out and causing me to crash."

The police officer asked the patient if he could describe the "yob" who had thrown the stone and was surprised that not only could Mr Johnson not describe the offender, but had not seen anyone at all. However, this didn't stop Mr Johnson from saying that he wanted the "yob caught and brought to justice". Mr Johnson stated emphatically that he had many "friends in high places", was a personal friend of the local MP and also played golf with several top barristers. He was sure that lots of 'ordinary' people were jealous of his new top of the range Mercedes, and wanted to cause damage to it.

By the time that he had finished giving his short statement to the police, Mr Johnson was red faced with anger and was only one step away from demanding the death penalty for all unemployed, single men living on a council estate who dared to show envy of him, his car and his lifestyle!

The police officer said that they would investigate the incident as fully as possible and left Mr Johnson in the capable hands of the A/E staff who set about cleaning and stitching the 6cm wound to his head.

Just over an hour later the same police constable returned to the department to update the patient on the investigation, and the police certainly hadn't been idle. The damaged Mercedes had been taken to the police garage, where the interior had been searched for the stone, or small rock, that Mr Johnson insisted had been thrown through his sunroof and struck him on the crown of his balding pate. Notwithstanding the fantastically good aim, or sheer luck involved in propelling a small missile through the relatively small sunroof of a vehicle travelling at 40mph, the police were mystified as to how the alleged 'yob' had managed to throw the stone at the car without being seen by Mr Johnson or the driver of the car that was travelling behind him.

On examination, the inside of the car was devoid of any stones, rocks or even pieces of gravel (which can certainly hurt if they strike you at 40mph), although the police officer examining the car did find one extraneous item on the front passenger seat – a large horse chestnut. The leafy lane that Mr Johnson was driving home along that afternoon was lined with magnificent mature oak and horse chestnut trees and in those trees lived various cute squirrels.

The general consensus amongst the police officers investigating the collision involving the Mercedes and the tree appeared to be that the movement of the squirrels through the branches probably shook the chestnut free from the tree which then fell into the car, through the sunroof, and bounced off Mr Johnson's head before coming to rest on the passenger seat. Surprised and momentarily stunned by the 'assault', Mr Johnson lost control of his car, which veered across the road and into one of the many large oak trees that had stood in the same spot for tens, if not hundreds, of years.

Relaying this proposed scenario to Mr Johnson, the police officer did a very good job of keeping a straight face whilst the gentleman continued to rage about the errant ways of the "youth of today". Taking advantage of the few moments in which Mr Johnson paused for breath, the officer reiterated that the accident appeared to have been caused by nothing more than a frisky squirrel and a rogue chestnut. Nonetheless, Mr Johnson continued to insist that someone be brought to book for the damage to his precious car.

"Tell you what sir," said the police officer, "I shall send an officer out to the location of the accident and we shall arrest any squirrels that are not going about their business in a lawful manner."

Incredibly, Mr Johnson accepted this proposal with a grunt of satisfaction and left the department in a taxi mollified that 'something was going to be done'!

Some patients arrive in Accident and Emergency alone, but are anxious to share their injury with friends, family and even friends of friends and slight acquaintances. The advent of the mobile phone or iPod with integral camera is a godsend for such patients. Usually young, and nearly always male, these patients often have photographs of their injury uploaded to facebook or other social networking sites before they have even been seen by a medical professional.

I called a young man into a cubicle with a presenting complaint of 'laceration to right leg'. Removing the grubby tea towel that he was holding to the limb I discovered a 5cm long laceration to his mid-thigh.

Apparently, whilst kneeling on the floor to cut a piece of carpet, the Stanley knife that he was using slipped and caused a cut to his upper leg. The laceration was quite deep and as it was in a meaty part of the body, fatty tissue was protruding from the wound. As I bent over the leg to assess the extent of the damage, the patient pulled out a mobile phone from his pocket and began snapping photographs of the injury.

"Nurse, can you take a picture for me?" he asked, handing me the phone and pulling the edges of the laceration further apart, causing further bleeding to a wound that had just started to heal itself. When I refused, he took the phone back from me and continued to take pictures.

Impatiently, I told him to put the phone away while I finished asking him questions and then I began to clean and treat the wound. After suturing the laceration, I put a dressing on it and made sure that the young man knew to keep the dressing clean and dry. I discharged him with the advice to keep an eye on the dressing, in case the wound should begin to bleed again and that if it should bleed through, to either go to the nurse at his local GP practice, or to return for me to re-dress it.

That should have been that, but just two hours after discharging him, my patient appeared back in the waiting room. Concerned, I went into the waiting room and called him through.

"Is it bleeding again?" I asked, thoroughly expecting that he had been taking the dressing off and interfering with the wound.

"Nah, it's fine," he said.

He reassured me that he had not touched the dressing since I had put it in place and, indeed, it was still as pristine as when first applied.

Confused, I asked him why he had returned.

"It's my girlfriend," he answered. "When she looked at the pictures of my cut she fainted and hit her head on the radiator. She's got a cut of her own on the side of her head. It's a real beauty but she won't let me take any photos of it!"

When in an enclosed cubicle, it can be easy to forget that the 'walls' between patient trolleys are in fact flimsy curtains and not solid bricks and mortar. Obviously this also means that although the cubicles may offer visual privacy, each and every sound uttered can be heard outside the immediate patient area, whether the curtains are closed or not. Quite often patients and relatives will forget that that they can be heard and that the 'if you can't see me, you also can't hear me' rule of childhood does not exist.

A couple of months ago, a young man was brought in by ambulance having driven his car into a lamp post. He had already been breathalysed by the police who had been convinced that he was drink driving, as a witness reported him swerving all over the road prior to the collision. The breath test was negative and the young man was making a big fuss about the loose dog that he had swerved to miss. He was not travelling very fast and could give the attending police officer a full description of the offending canine.

As the young man was brought in to the department strapped to a spinal board with a hard collar on as a precaution against neck/spinal injuries, the police officer promised to return after the required examination and x-rays to get a formal statement. The lad was adamant that he was not at fault and, in fact, had done the dog a good turn by not hitting it!

When he later mentioned that it was his mother's relatively new car that he had damaged and that she would, in his words, "go nuts", we all began to feel quite sorry for him and, in fact, one of the nurses offered to phone his mum to give her the news, therefore making it a little easier on him. That was until he had been examined and x-rayed and then left in the cubicle, with the curtains closed, to phone his friend for a lift home. The entire conversation could be heard quite clearly on the other side of the curtains and the call went something as follows:

"Hi mate, yeah, guess what happened to me? So, like I was really busy tweeting, and then, like BOOM! I drove into this lamp post or something. My mum's new car is a real mess with the bumper off and everything. It's ok though because I spun them a tale about a stray dog, which even the copper believed, and now they all feel sorry for me. They're even gonna get me off the hook with my mum. I love Twitter. It's like, so crazy. Can you come and pick me up? Oh yeah, and when you get here, just mention to the nurses about what a big dog lover I am or something. It'll just prove my story."

Needless to say, following this conversation, all sympathy went out of the window, he was instructed to phone his own mother and 'fess up', and the conversation was repeated to the police officer on his return!

≈ 36 ≈

Induction

When starting work in St Joseph's, no matter what ward or department you are working in, everybody has to go through the dreaded 'induction'. This consists of several days of being crammed into a small classroom listening to lectures about Health and Safety, Fire training, policies and procedures, and other such mind numbing material. Depending on the area of expertise in which you worked, some members of staff got away without having to attend the patient handling based lectures – but being at 'the sharp end' in Accident and Emergency, we got the lot.

One of the training days 'to be attended by all staff' is the fire safety training. This involves the boring 'in the classroom' bit, followed by the part where we were allowed out onto the lawn to practice letting off various fire extinguishers. The idea behind this was to be able to establish which type of extinguisher to use for different types of fires and to learn how to handle and hold them correctly. Unfortunately, put a group of bored adults in charge of objects that spray pressurised water at the touch of a button (or pull of a lever) and there's bound to be trouble. Many utterances of "Ooh I'm sorry", "whoops, must be the wind" and "I didn't realise they'd be as difficult to handle" were heard as water and foam sprayed around the area, covering a good few people in the process.

It was a hot day in July at the start of my induction week and I was sharing a classroom with at least twelve other people. The two small windows in the classroom were open to their fullest extent but that did not relieve the stuffiness of the room, or the obnoxious smell of body odour from the sweating, overweight man who had just taken a job in the pharmacy department and had settled his bulk at the desk next to mine. The motley crew of new recruits were from various wards and departments and included a gentleman wearing a turban, a male healthcare assistant who fairly minced around the room, a black girl in her twenties, two older looking ladies and three other men and three women – together we looked more like the cast of a politically correct banking advert than the newest members of staff at a busy general hospital.

The Fire Training began with a lecture on what to do if the fire alarm sounded and how to evacuate the hospital. We had just been told that under no circumstances were the lifts to be used in the event of an evacuation and that our personal safety was paramount.

"What about the patients on life support machines in the intensive care unit?" asked a young girl sitting near the back. She had just acquired a position nursing in the ICU, and as it was situated on the third floor of the main building, hers was a valid question. The lifts were out of bounds, there were at least six flights of stairs down from the intensive care unit, and most of the patients were dependent upon machines to keep them alive.

"The main thing is that you make sure that you are safe." she was told.

The young lady was aghast.

"You mean we just ..... leave them?" she asked. "We leave them to burn to a crisp in their beds? Just in the place where they are supposed to be safe, where we are charged with making them well and helping them to get home to their families?" Her eyes began to well with tears. "I can't do that," she said.

Personally, I gave her three weeks in the realities of the job before she was either the first one out of the door should the fire alarm sound, or she suffered from a total breakdown.

Health and Safety training was as boring as anticipated, and emphasised the importance of 'the correct tools for the job'. I could just imagine the faces of the staff involved in a full blown resuscitation who had asked me to reach a size 6.5 endotracheal tube down from the shelf (a breathing tube that is placed into the throat to attach to a ventilator in order to 'breathe' for the unconscious patient) if I said that I was not allowed to stand on the chair directly in front of me in order to reach the shelf, but if they'd just hang on for a few minutes or so, I'd go down the corridor to the store cupboard and see if there was an appropriately sized step ladder that I might use in order to reach the shelf safely!

There was only one slightly exciting part of the week (and I use the term 'exciting' in the context of a whole week of lectures about payroll and deductions from our pay; making sure that we knew that if we *must* vomit during a messy resuscitation then to do it away from patient areas; and the hierarchical structure of the National Health Service). The only session some of us were at all looking forward to was the "Handling Violence and Aggression in the NHS" lecture. This was mainly because it was to be given by a bronzed and muscular young man who looked like a male model. The session was aimed at those of us dealing with difficult or confused patients on a day to day basis, and the main theme of the session was avoiding conflict and defusing potentially threatening situations.

The man giving the talk strode into the room wearing a pair of *very* tight jeans, a clinging vest type sleeveless tee-shirt, and spent the whole time rubbing his biceps or playing with his nipples – and gave the entire lecture to the cleavage of the young lady sitting in the front row.

"But what if someone just *comes* at me?" asked the effeminate young man after a lesson on how to run away gracefully, without looking as though we were running away at all.

I could understand his predicament: he stood all of five foot five and looked as though he weighed a maximum of nine stone soaking wet. Unfortunately, he was also one of those people who had a natural whine to their voice, and he irritated me as soon as he opened his mouth.

"Come here." said the lecturer.

Apparently the Chippendale used to be in the armed forces but had since left, presumably because it didn't allow him to display his more sadistic side to its best advantage. I also got the distinct impression that the effeminate chap irritated him just as much, if not more, than he did me.

As the young man minced towards the lecturer, he was grabbed, spun around and left fighting for air with his nose shoved into the armpit of the grinning lecturer. As the poor man turned beet red and then began to show a bluish tinge to his skin, he was abruptly dropped to the floor.

Seeing that he had suitably wowed the female members of the room by suffocating a much smaller, weaker man, he ended his lecture by flashing up seventies style pictures of bearded men and blonde ladies grappling around on the floor, which all looked as though they had been lifted directly from a 1970s sex manual.

"This one," he intoned, "has to be done surreptitiously, because by law, it doesn't constitute 'reasonable force' ."

"The main thing is," he continued, "if the patient is drunk, you can do just about anything, providing no-one sees you, and providing that he doesn't know your name. Everyone knows that drunks can't remember diddly-squat and, anyway, you can always deny it and say that he must have dreamed or imagined whatever happened."

The young lady from the Intensive Care Unit was sitting at the back of the room with her mouth open, and at the last comment I heard her gasp.

"It's alright, love," said the hunk, "Your patients won't be drunk and won't be a problem to you. It's the *relatives* that you've got to watch out for."

There was actually a large element of truth to this, as relatives of seriously ill patients can become quite upset and lash out at whoever is giving them the bad news, and usually that is the doctor or nurse standing in the same room. This anger is a quite understandable reaction, especially from the relatives of those patients suddenly involved in an accident or incident that leaves them fighting for their life.

"Oh, that's ok," said the young lady, "the relatives of *my* patients will be fine. I'll just sit quietly with them whilst I explain that their family member is dangerously unwell, and then offer to pray with them."

Oh dear. I revised my original estimate, and concluded that if the young lady lasted for more than a full week in her new job, then she was doing well.

At the end of the week, we had all gained a thick wad of papers full of 'do's and don'ts' but, if the rest of the new staff were anything like me, they only remembered a tiny portion of what we had been told.

≈ *37* ≈

AWOL

We use many different types of medication in
Accident and Emergency, but my favourite drug
ever must be Naloxone (also known as Narcan).
Naloxone is a drug given to counteract the effects of opiates
such as heroin and morphine, and is given as an antidote to
patients that have taken an opiate overdose. The biggest worry
with these patients is the life threatening respiratory
depression that can cause them to stop breathing altogether,
and this reversal agent prevents that from happening.

Naloxone is fast acting, and I mean FAST acting. It is
given intravenously and works within sixty seconds of being
given. The patients that Naloxone is given to are, by their very
nature, not very happy people and these people usually wake
up rather unhappy too. A patient can go from being
unconscious and barely breathing to sitting up and lashing out
with fists within seconds.

It takes experience to know how much Naloxone to give
in one dose and to spot the very first signs that the patient
may be recovering, and most of us have gained our experience
the hard way.

Sebastian had been with us as a junior doctor for two
months. During that time he had established himself amongst
the team as a young man who had been there, done that and
got the tee-shirt. Sebastian was the product of a rather

exclusive private school followed by a top university education. He had begun his medical career in one of the large London teaching hospitals and then decided to follow his girlfriend to St Joseph's where he joined us on a six month rotation as a senior house officer.

Unfortunately, Sebastian was not the type of man to take advice and when a muscular young man in his late twenties came in following a suspected heroin overdose, Sebastian was keen to give the medication that would reverse the sedative effects. One of the staff nurses began drawing up the Naloxone and asked Sebastian if he had administered the stuff before.

"What does that matter?" he retorted

Jayne began to explain the speed at which the drug worked, only to have Sebastian speak over her in a condescending tone.

"I do have a *medical* degree in *medicine*, nurse." he said. "That's why I'm qualified to give *medicines* to real live people."

Jayne opened her mouth to speak again and then decided against it.

Handing the syringe of Naloxone to Sebastian, she readjusted the oxygen mask on her patient and then very carefully took several steps back.

Sebastian located the cannula in the man's left hand, placed there by the paramedics who had collected him, and injected the full dose.

In almost the blink of an eye, the man was struggling to sit up and flailing his arms about.

Sebastian was still faffing about at the side of the trolley, and just as Jayne spoke his name in warning, the patient leaned over and smacked him open handed right across the bridge of his nose. As the doctor reeled backwards bleeding from both nostrils, the patient yanked his oxygen mask off, and in one movement pulled off the blood pressure cuff that was encircling his right arm and scooted to the end of the trolley.

It took him all of ten seconds to be on his feet and staggering towards the double doors in the resuscitation room. This was not done in silence, and in the time that it took him to get to the door, both Sebastian and Jayne were treated to a constant barrage of profanity and verbal attacks on their characters and personal appearances.

One of the first things that we do when a patient arrives in the resuscitation room is to strip off their clothing. This is done in order for us to have full access to any part of the body for the purposes of full examination and for us to have a clear field in which to place our various monitoring devices and electrodes. This is especially important if we have a patient in a state of collapse who cannot explain why he has attended.

Charlie, having being brought by ambulance virtually unconscious, had been fully undressed and was sporting a rather fetching hospital gown – flapping open at the back, as we had left it untied so that we could keep monitoring electrodes on his chest to ensure a constant readout of his heart's activity. Beneath the short and revealing gown he had nothing on: his underpants had been removed as they had become soiled at some point during Charlie's collapse.

So there he stood, pushing frantically at the door marked 'Pull', with his bare, pimply buttocks waving about in the breeze. Almost as soon as the word 'pull' registered in his befuddled mind, he had yanked on the door handle and scarpered through the door. The double doors of the resuscitation room led into a small lobby area, which were headed by a another pair of doors, this time automatic ones which slid open, revealing the car park beyond.

Within a moment or two he was gone from view, and looking round the room, Jayne saw Sebastian peeking from around the corner where the portable x-ray machine was kept.

"Has he gone?" he asked plaintively "Bit cross wasn't he?"

The hospital now had a problem. Not only had a patient gone AWOL but he was to all intents and purposes buck naked, and it was a cold November day. Added to that was the fact that the Naloxone that Sebastian had given has a much shorter half-life than the opiates that Charlie had originally taken, and so would wear off a lot faster, leaving the patient back in the state that he had arrived in in the first place.

Sighing, Jayne began making the phone calls and filling out the forms that are necessary when a patient decides to do a runner. She started off by phoning the security office and speaking to one of the three security men that work for the hospital.

I say security, but in fact these gentlemen were partly employed as car park attendants and partly as security guards – and all three looked as if stopping a five year old in his tracks would give them bother.

One of the men was an ex prison officer. Ex was the operative word, as he had retired from the prison service nigh on twenty years ago and was easily seventy years of age. Walking around the car park and giving out tickets was Norman's forte; running after virtually naked escaped junkies? – no chance.

Working alongside Norman was Howard. Howard was at least forty years younger than Norman, and fifteen stone heavier. Howard could not match Norman as he strode around the car park. For every step taken by Norman, Howard managed two, with a few moments rest every couple of hundred yards or so.

Howard had a permanently red face and probably had dangerously high blood pressure. The thought of either of these men being able to catch a fit looking man in his twenties with a strong desire to escape, was laughable. Just a slight quickening of his step was enough to bring Howard out in a sweat and should he have to run anywhere, he would probably end up as a patient himself, occupying a bed in the cardiac care unit.

Nevertheless, Jayne did her duty and left a description of the man with the security officers. Next, she phoned the hospital manager, and then followed it up with a call to the police as she was worried about Charlie's general state of health.

The police control officer taking the call sounded bored as she took down the few details that Jayne could offer. They knew that his name was Charlie, courtesy of the acquaintance that had been good enough to call an ambulance for him and then wait around just long enough for the paramedics to attend. That, and his personal description, was just about all the information that the hospital had about him. He had been picked up in the doorway of Woolworths on the high street and had no identification on him at all. No surname, no address and certainly no telephone number. Asking for a description of his clothing, Jayne replied that he was wearing a hospital gown, emblazoned with the words 'hospital property' in yellow and red and with two little tie-ups at the back, and nothing else. The police control officer perked up a little at this.

"REALLY naked." she said. "As in no underwear beneath it. Wow." And then, a bit unnecessarily, "But it's winter, he'll catch a cold."

Explaining that feeling a bit cold was soon to be the least of Charlie's problems, and if he wasn't found fairly soon, then he could quite possibly never, ever feel anything ever again, the police control officer promised to send "an officer or two" to look for him.

It took just another half an hour before a second ambulance brought Charlie back for another visit. He had been found twenty minutes up the road inside McDonald's. Feeling a little cold, he had gone into the restaurant to warm up and collapsed almost as soon as he entered the establishment. Obviously the Naloxone was wearing off. Interestingly, despite his state of obvious undress, bare feet and dried blood on his arm where he had pulled out his cannula, no-one had thought to contact the police as he walked the twenty minutes along a busy dual carriageway, through the town centre and into McDonald's before collapsing. The manager of McDonald's only thought to contact an ambulance when he eventually collapsed because "he hadn't ordered anything and we were getting near to lunchtime and he was getting in the way"!

This time, Charlie wasn't going anywhere. In collapsing the second time he had landed with his foot caught underneath him and from the looks of it now had a broken, or at least, a very badly sprained ankle into the bargain, and the paramedics had done an excellent job in placing a rigid vacuum splint on his right lower leg, effectively scuppering any further chance of making a run for it.

This time, Sebastian heeded Jayne's advice and gave a smaller dose in increments, whilst carefully watching for signs of recovery in between.

In this job, we all live and learn.

≈ 38 ≈

A Debt of Gratitude

One big rule of working within the hospital Trust is that as staff we cannot accept personal gifts from patients, or from their relatives. Those grateful patients that insist on giving a financial reward to the nurses are asked to donate it to the department coffee fund so that the proceeds can be shared throughout the whole department. Most patients are quite au fait with the fact that we are not supposed to accept monetary contributions and at least once a week, we receive a tin of biscuits or box of chocolates as a 'thank you' gift. These are always gratefully received and go a long way to boosting the blood sugars of the poor staff members that have missed out on their coffee/lunch break that day.

Gifts also come in the form of teabags, jars of coffee and, a personal favourite; home-made cakes.

One weekday morning, a delightful elderly lady was brought in by her daughter after catching her leg on the corner of a cupboard. She had fragile skin and the simple brush past the sharp wooden corner had resulted in a 'v' shaped tear to the skin of her lower leg. This was known as a 'skinflap' laceration and is exactly as it sounds – a torn flap of skin hanging down from a usually shallow cut. Skinflap lacerations are quite common in elderly patients, or patients with thinner skin, and are quite time consuming to repair.

The repair is effected by painstakingly rolling the flap of skin back over the wound with a damp cotton bud and then steri-stripping it back in place. These are very rewarding wounds to treat, as a really nasty looking wound can be transformed back into a reasonably looking limb with just a few strips of sticky paper and a lot of concentration.

One of our Emergency Nurse Practitioners was a bit of an expert on skin flap repairs and prided himself on his repair to Mrs Hobbs' leg. After spending close to an hour painstakingly bent over her wound, her leg began to look an awful lot better. Finishing off her care with a neat bandage, he discharged her back home with instructions to keep the dressing clean and dry and to keep the leg rested.

The following day the same patient returned to the department, only this time she was bearing a large Tupperware box containing savoury biscuits.

Usually even a large box of biscuits can be finished off within a single day, but, apart from one of the doctors and two of the nursing staff, most people found the biscuits a bit dry. They were best eaten dunked in a cup of tea or coffee, which softened them up a bit.

A few days later the lady came back requesting that we check and redress her wound as she couldn't get an appointment with the nurse at her GP surgery.

"I bet you've already eaten my biscuits," she said "they're my favourites, I love them."

Not wanting to offend her, Gareth stated that although he really liked them, they were a bit different from a lot of the usual, generic biscuits that we have in the staff room.

"Well that's because technically they are dog biscuits, but I think that I eat more than little Sophie, because she's not too keen on them." she said. "I buy two boxes a week."

From then on, Gareth became known as 'Mrs Hobbs' pet doggy' and for many months, became the butt of every canine style joke known to man!

Even more unusual gifts to the department have been the bag containing sample sized tubes of toothpaste brought in by the dental hygienist for the night staff, and a case of a dozen bottles of still water donated by a drinks rep because "not everyone drinks tea or coffee."

I think, though, that by far the worst thing given to me was handed over by a gentleman in the triage room. He came in clutching a plastic Marks and Spencer carrier bag and stating that he had got an "infected foot".

Removing the shoe and sock from his right foot, he shoved his toes under my nose and said "It's totally infected you know."

A little confused, I answered that the foot looked all right to me, and asked him why he thought that it was infected.

"I was walking barefoot in *my* front garden," he said "When I stood right in the middle of a turd. It squidged right between my toes, and I got bits of it under my big toe nail," he said.

After a full explanation of just how "squidgy" the offending stool was (as if I really wanted to know), the gentleman then delivered a five minute rant of how it was left by the "flea ridden mongrel" next door on one of its regular escape missions.

The upshot of this explanation, was that he was sure that his foot must be infected because the dog itself was "probably full of diseases and parasites". He slammed the plastic bag down on the triage desk, treating me to a large waft of 'odour de dog poo'.

"I want this turd tested." he said "I need to know what bugs I've got on my foot so that you can treat it before it gets gangrenous and drops off."

I explained that, as an Accident and Emergency department we treat *accidents* and *emergencies* and, funnily enough, the testing of dog poo does not fall into either category. After another long rant, the man finally got up to leave, but asked me to "keep the turd in case I get time to do something with it." After all, he said, he had gone to the effort of scraping it off his foot and putting into the bag for me in the first place.

I so wish he hadn't made the effort.

That same week another middle aged gentleman arrived in the triage room stating that he had been "abducted by aliens, who probed my rectum". He had brought along a small sandwich bag containing a clear jelly like substance, and announced that he had "got their DNA" and wanted us to test it to ensure that they had not left any alien parasites inside him.

The mind boggles.

≈ 39 ≈

Dem Bones

A few weeks ago I had lost two patients by eleven o'clock in the morning – and I wasn't the only one. Another nurse had lost an elderly male patient and the consultant on duty that day had lost three! All of these patients had been lost in the true sense of the word. They had been given x-ray forms, directed towards the x-ray department and then asked to return after having their picture taken, to be seen by the doctor that had originally examined them.

None of them had come back. This was really odd as the x-ray department is situated right next to the Accident and Emergency department and was reached by going through a pair of double doors at the far end of the department.

Ambulant patients were given their x-ray request forms and directed to the correct department. They had just to go through the double doors, walk through the x-ray department waiting room and to the reception desk situated at the other side of the department, next to another set of doors that led out onto the main corridor and into the rest of the hospital.

Deciding to try and find out what had happened to our missing patients, I set off into the x-ray department myself. Crossing the waiting room, I noticed that the usual sign simply reading "X-ray Department" had gone, to be replaced by a sign hanging from the ceiling reading "Department of

Diagnostic Imaging". Approaching the receptionist, I asked her if she had seen any of our missing patients.

Checking the records, she confirmed that none of the patients that I had named had booked in for an x-ray that morning, although she did comment that an awful lot of people seemed to be using the x-ray department as a short cut to the main hospital corridor that day. Among them were several people limping and an elderly gentleman in a wheelchair being pushed by a relative.

Having neither the energy nor the inclination to go searching further, I came to the conclusion that the missing patients would eventually find their way back to the A/E department and they would then be redirected to have their x-ray taken at the *Department of Diagnostic Imaging.*

Within a couple of days, two new signs had appeared next to the Diagnostic Imaging Sign – one stating Magnetic Resonance Imaging and the other for the Computerised Axial Tomography scan room. Great: now the outpatients attending for an MRI or CT scan are set to get just as confused.

I waited with bated breath for the next batch of signs to arrive, perhaps directing the way to the "Department of Urinary and Faecal Elimination" or the "Department of Nutrition and Hydration". They have yet to appear, but I am sure that it is only a matter of time.

The yellow x-ray forms given in to the x-ray department, excuse me, the *Diagnostic Imaging Department*, have several boxes for the examining doctor or nurse to fill in. These consist of the expected name, address, date of birth and GP details, along with a larger box for the 'mechanism of injury'. This is a very important section as it gives the radiographer an idea as to the type and severity of the injury. Each health professional has their own way of filling out the forms; some will write reams of unnecessary information, whilst others insist on simple one liners.

Once a week, for a few hours in the afternoon, all of the junior doctors have a teaching session held by one of the consultants, and in their place we have two local GPs in order to ensure that we still have doctors on 'the shop floor'. One of these GPs, pleasant though he is, appears to be on a mission to do as little work as he can get away with, and this included his form filling.

More than once, we have had an irate radiographer stride into the department waving a yellow x-ray form and demanding to know why there was virtually no information on it.

One Tuesday afternoon, Dr Cromer sent another two patients to x-ray, and lo and behold, as if on cue, a red faced radiographer appeared in the doctors' office demanding that the x-ray request forms be filled out correctly. Not only does the correct filling out of these forms help the radiographers in their job, but they are also a legal document, something that the radiographer was keen to impress upon Dr Cromer.

Heaving a dramatic sigh, the doctor duly filled out the forms with the correct information whilst muttering under his breath that the radiographer was "wasting his time".

A few hours later, a second radiographer appeared in the department asking to see Dr Cromer. She was interested as to his explanation of the form accompanying the patient with a suspected broken wrist that was explained as "a lost argument with something more solid than bone" and the probable fractured ankle that was merely explained as "looks broken to me"! Unfortunately, the poor radiographers were fighting a losing battle as, despite their best efforts, Dr Cromer's form filling never did improve.

One Saturday, among what appeared to be dozens of football related injuries, we had a young lad attend with a painful ankle injury. He was brought in by his football coach and as one of the Senior House Officers examined the ten year old, in order to help encourage his cooperation, he began a conversation about football.

"What team do you support then?" asked George.

The lad replied that he supported Liverpool FC and then proceeded to wax lyrical about the merits of Ryan Babel and Steven Gerrard and the fact that he wanted to be a great player just like them.

"Who do you support?" asked the lad.

George stated that he wasn't a big football fan but he did follow Chelsea when he was younger.

"Chelsea suck," said the lad. "Ancelotti hasn't got a clue."

Realising that he was probably getting onto shaky ground, and to keep the child's interest, George said that the radiographers in the x-ray department normally only x-ray Chelsea supporters on Saturdays. and Liverpool supporters get x-rayed on Sundays.

"But they're going to make an exception for you today," he said, "because you have been so well behaved."

The child duly had his film taken, which showed a small, undisplaced fracture that was treated with a plaster cast.

Normally, that would be that, but George wasn't sure whether to be amused or appalled when a letter of complaint arrived in the department from the mother of the young boy. The letter contained the complaint that the doctor that had treated her son had discriminated against him because he wasn't a Chelsea supporter, and had arranged to "change the rules" in order to have his ankle x-rayed. Her main complaint was that "if that doctor hadn't been on duty, he would have had to wait until Sunday for an x-ray, which wasn't satisfactory as Liam was in a great deal of pain".

Sometimes being friendly to a patient can backfire.

Generally, while treating a patient, a bit of friendly conversation can help. It not only relaxes the patient a little but it is a way of gaining further information around the injury or illness that may not have been offered during the initial consultation.

Cleaning and dressing the self-inflicted wound on the forearm of an eighteen year old girl one day, I noticed from her notes that she had a birthday due the following Saturday. I asked her if she had any plans to celebrate her birthday.

"No." she said. She lived alone, she added. I asked if she had parents or siblings to share the day with.

She replied that her mother was dead.

I sympathised and said "How about your dad?"

"He's in prison." she said.

Curious, but not heeding my inner voice to change the subject, I asked if he was in prison for a long time.

"I damn well hope so," she said. "He killed my mum."

OK. This was now a tad awkward and I struggled to steer the conversation towards a better subject.

"How about brothers or sisters?" I said "Or friends? Surely you have someone who would like to share a drink with you?"

"I'm an only child." she stated "Just as well really because my parents were crap at parenting. My so-called best friend has just moved in with my now EX-boyfriend after I caught them having sex in our bed last week, and our friends were exactly that: OUR friends, so really they're just *his* friends now. Besides which, I'm sure that they all knew that he was seeing Katie a long time before I caught them at it."

I now felt really sorry for the poor girl, and deeply regretted even mentioning her birthday.

"Anyway, I don't drink anymore" she continued "my counsellor got me in an AA group because the cheap cider was messing with my head."

Eighteen years old, a recovering alcoholic with no friends, no family to speak of and a boyfriend that had done the ultimate dirty on her. No wonder that she felt the need to self-harm and I silently counted my blessings for a somewhat 'normal' life, at the same time reminding myself to keep the conversation to inoffensive subjects like the weather, or gardening.

≈ 40 ≈

Complaints

I f you've worked anywhere for any length of time, at some point a complaint of some sort, justified or not, is likely to be made about you. Whether it is from a patient, a relative or a colleague, it's bound to happen. Most complaints come about because the patient (or relative) "knows their rights" and is aware of the governments targets ensuring that patients have to be seen, treated and discharged within a four hour time frame. Hence if someone is still waiting to be seen after four hours, they tend to "want something done about it".

The introduction of this government target was a good idea because it drastically reduced the amount of patients that were hanging around in the Accident and Emergency Department for hours and hours and ensured that the corridors were no longer full of patients waiting on trolleys to be seen – sometimes for six hours plus. The down side of this target time was that it was a blanket four hours – with very few exceptions – and as people are individuals and some people take longer to treat, or maybe need a little longer to recover, there were a lot of patients being discharged 'on paper' at 3 hours and 59 minutes, when in fact they were still very much in the department and hadn't actually gone anywhere. In fact, patients like Mrs Barry sometimes remained in the department for nearer five hours out of necessity, but the paperwork resolutely stated that she was discharged home at exactly 3 hours and 59 minutes.

Mrs Barry was a lady in her late eighties and had come into Accident and Emergency after being knocked over by her little Yorkshire Terrier, Timmy.

Mrs Barry lived alone with Timmy and walked around her small bungalow with a pair of walking sticks. One afternoon Timmy had dashed across the room just as his mistress was getting up and, getting tangled between her legs knocked one walking stick to the floor. This caused Mrs Barry to fall forward onto her outstretched hand, and the result was a nasty Colles fracture to the right wrist. (A Colles fracture is a particular type of fracture that causes the bones of the wrist to also become displaced. The wrist takes on a certain deformity known as a 'dinner fork' deformity, due to the fact that it looks like the bend in the neck of a table fork.)

A Colles fracture is particularly painful and immediate treatment in A&E is required to pull the bones back into position to prevent permanent damage to the hand. This is usually effected by giving the patient a heavy sedative and strong pain relief directly into a vein and then the attending doctor will manipulate the broken bones back into position while another doctor or nurse provides counter-traction on the upper limb. Once back into position a plaster cast can then be applied to ensure that the bones stay in place.

The amount of sedation and pain relief required varies greatly from patient to patient, and as Mrs Barry was quite an elderly lady, and quite petite too, a quarter sized dose was first given to see how she would react.

This appeared to have no effect at all, and Mrs Barry said that she felt absolutely no different following the injection. After a few minutes of waiting, the doctor injected a little more of the sedative. Still no effect. In fact Mrs Barry was getting rather anxious now, and kept asking whether we were giving her the correct medication. Reassuring her that we were, indeed, giving her the correct stuff, she was given just another 2mls of the sedative (less than half a teaspoon) and she suddenly announced "I feel funny", as her head lolled forward – and she stopped breathing.

Jumping into action, an airway was placed into her throat and an ambubag employed to help push air into her lungs. At the same time, the doctor was already preparing the reversal agent that he needed to inject as an antidote to the sedative. Within a few minutes he had given the drug and she was breathing again, but still out for the count.

Swiftly, he realigned her wrist bones and we placed a solid plaster cast on the lower arm.

It was now 4pm and Mrs Barry had arrived by ambulance at just gone 1 o'clock. On arrival, she had gone directly into the department where she had been examined, given pain relief and sent for an x-ray. Following this, she had to wait for the x-ray results and then for the doctor to come and see her to explain that she had broken her wrist, and what we were going to do about it. She then had to wait for a second member of staff to be free, for the doctor to give the necessary drugs, and for him to manipulate the wrist. There was now less than an hour left before her four hour time limit was up, and she was fast asleep and snoring like a pneumatic drill.

It took another hour before the lady was sufficiently awake to comprehend where she was and remember why she was in hospital. During this time, a kindly neighbour had arrived to take her home and stay with her overnight, and eventually, at 5.45pm, Mrs Barry had had a cup of tea and a piece of toast, and was steady enough on her feet to be discharged home.

Had she been discharged any earlier, she certainly would not have been safe and might quite possibly have returned later on following another fall as she was so unsteady on her legs. Nevertheless, the computer stated that she had fully recovered and was on her way home at exactly 3 hours and 59 minutes!

One day, a letter of complaint reached the Matron's desk, and I was invited into her office to read it. It went something like this:

"Dear Matron,
Last Tuesday one of our elderly residents was admitted to your Accident and Emergency Department. She came in by ambulance and was admitted by one of the staff nurses. When she was admitted, Mrs Bamber was wearing a pink nightdress with three buttons on the front and embroidered roses on the collar. Unfortunately, while in your care, one of the nurses ruined Mrs Bamber's nightdress, which is now unwearable. As she has no family, one of the residential home staff bought this nightdress for Mrs Bamber for Christmas and we are all very upset at the fact that it is now wrecked.

We would be grateful if you could please reprimand the nurse that ruined Mrs Bamber's nightdress and ensure that it does not happen again. Financial recompense for the cost of the garment would be appreciated."

This was then signed by the lady in charge of the residential home that Mrs Bamber had been admitted from.

Mrs Bamber had been my patient, and I was the big bad nurse that had "ruined her nightdress".

One Friday morning, a patient came into the resuscitation room with a history of collapsing whilst using the commode in the residential home in which she lived. This patient was 88 years old, suffered from dementia and was unconscious. The paramedics had done a good job in inserting a cannula and had delivered her to the resuscitation room within fifteen minutes of collecting her from her home.

As Mrs Bamber was placed onto the trolley in the department, she took a deep breath, opened her eyes and said "My chest hurts."

At the same time, her skin colour turned grey and she lapsed back into unconsciousness. Realising that she might have suffered a cardiac arrest – a life threatening medical emergency whereby the heart ceases to beat effectively – we needed immediate access to her chest in order to attach the ECG heart tracing leads and to place the pads in case we had to use the cardiac defibrillator.

Luckily, as it was early morning, the only clothing that Mrs Bamber was wearing was a thin nylon nightdress and it took just seconds for me to run my scissors straight up the centre of the garment.

We immediately checked the patient's heart rhythm, and realizing that she did indeed require the use of the defibrillator, administered the necessary shocks. To everyone's great relief, the heart monitor began to show a more normal rhythm and Mrs Bamber's colour started to improve.

After a couple of hours of monitoring and treatment, Mrs Bamber was improved enough to leave the department and to be admitted to the Coronary Care Unit.

One of the disadvantages of working in the Accident and Emergency department is that our patients are only with us for a few hours (or '3 hours and 59 minutes' if they are particularly ill). Either way, they are then discharged into the general hospital populace and we lose track of them. This can be very frustrating as sometimes it would be good to know how some of our patients have fared.

Knowing that Mrs Bamber had gone to the Coronary Care Unit meant that I could keep track of her progress a little more easily and I was pleased to learn that after just five days of staying in CCU she was well enough to be discharged back to her residential home.

A few days later, the letter from the residential home arrived on Matrons desk. After running through an explanation of the course of events, I asked Matron if I could reply to the letter myself. Surprisingly enough, I was given permission to do so, but with the proviso that the reply was vetted by Matron herself before it was sent.

Fair enough. I spent the next weekend formulating a firm but polite reply and handed it to Matron on Monday morning for her to read. It took her all of five minutes to read it through and refuse me permission to send it on. Personally, I could not see the problem. I had explained to the person in charge of the residential home why I had cut off the lady's nightdress and gone into detail as to why I had had to do so as a matter of urgency. I deliberately hadn't mentioned the fact that it was a cheap and nasty nightdress that had definitely seen better days, or the fact that it was actually quite badly soiled already following the patients sudden collapse. I think, though, that the phrase that condemned my letter was when I explained to the lady in charge that if preferred, in future, I would ensure that any patient who was unfortunate enough to be seriously ill was admitted from that particular residential home would be carefully undressed and their clothing folded and put to one side. The clothing could then be given back to the home in pristine condition and they could decide what to do with it after they had visited the patient in the mortuary.

As it was, instead, a response was sent by the powers that be – pen-pushers who have no idea what it is like to work at 'the sharp end'. They sent a bunch of flowers to the patient concerned and a letter of profuse apology on my behalf! At no point was I permitted to add an explanation (even a watered down, edited version) and I fumed for weeks over the injustice.

Usually, the patients that complain the loudest about waiting to be seen are those that do not need to be seen at all.

The patient waiting for three hours to be told that no, we do not do ear syringing in A&E, will probably have spent two and half of those three hours complaining about having to wait.

Some patients have got queue jumping down to a fine art. They know the 'buzz words' and are well aware that the words "chest pain" and/or "shortness of breath" will ensure that they are seen straight away. Of course, should it transpire that the 'chest pain' or 'breathlessness' has miraculously got better as soon as the patient is directed to a cubicle, then they may find that their wait suddenly becomes a bit more prolonged. Other patients may find that they are waiting for a much shorter time simply by courtesy of being part of 'the Great Unwashed'.

One afternoon, one of the receptionists came through to the main department from the waiting room. The reception desk is situated at one end of the waiting room and it appeared that a gentleman had booked himself into Accident and Emergency less than ten minutes ago. The patient himself was not concerned by the full waiting room, or the fact that the receptionist had told him that there was quite a long wait to be seen.

"That's fine, love." he said, and plonked himself down in a chair next to the reception desk.

Marta had come to speak to one of the nurses to see if we would push this new patient up a bit in time order.

Quite often, one of the receptionists will approach a member of nursing staff to say that a patient is now feeling more unwell, or, conversely, that they suddenly feel a lot better and have decided to go home without seeing a doctor (much more common on busy days with a heaving waiting room!). This was the first time that a receptionist had requested that we prioritise a patient that was quite happy to wait and was just complaining of a painful toe.

Somewhat confused, I asked if he was feeling sick.

No.

Was he feeling dizzy, or had he got severe pain?

No.

"Really though," said Marta "You've got to call him through, and now!"

I walked through to the waiting room in order to speak to the gentleman concerned. Although I could see him sitting there quite comfortably next to Marta's desk, I could smell him well before I got close.

The patient in question smelled very strongly of urine, and mixed in with this was the distinct smell of alcohol. Approaching as close as I dared, I looked down at the man, who was contentedly picking his nose with a long grimy fingernail.

"Got a bad toe, nurse." he said, as he continued with his digital exploration.

Realising that the chairs either side of him were empty, and the three chairs opposite him had been recently vacated, I looked around the waiting room to see several people perched on the arms of chairs, or sitting on the floor further into the room. The waiting room was full, but, understandably, the gentleman with the "bad toe" was sitting in glorious isolation with just Marta at the desk for company.

One of the other patients, a young lady, pulled me to one side.

"Please could you jump the queue with that man?" she asked "A few people have already left because of the smell and I swear I saw *things* jumping in his hair."

Now I was in quandary. Anything that encouraged people to leave without being seen was, in my book, a good idea. Especially as they probably weren't emergencies in the first place. On the other hand, this chap really was offensive and, looking over at him, I was sure that there probably <u>were</u> *things* in his hair, not to mention anywhere else.

Bearing in mind that the triage room was small and windowless, I made the decision to take the man directly into 'Minors'. Once ensconced in the far end cubicle, I asked him to remove his shoe and sock so that I could look at the offending toe.

Taking off his muddy shoe, he then leant down to his sock, but before actually removing it, he took out a half-eaten sandwich from the top and laid it carefully on the trolley next to him.

"Ham," he stated. "couldn't eat it all, so I've saved it until I'm hungry. Waste not, want not."

Supressing a shudder at what might be residing in the unwrapped sandwich, I asked to see his toe.

Concealed under many weeks of caked-in dirt, I could just make out a red and inflamed big toe, the result of his ingrowing toenail. I asked if he had seen his GP.

"No, love," he replied "They never have any appointments free for me."

Understanding completely and feeling a wee bit sorry for his GP, I cleaned and dressed his toe and advised that he make an appointment as soon as he got home.

"I'll try," he said, "but if I can't get an appointment I'll come back here. Great service. I hardly had to wait any time at all, and there's *loads* of people in the waiting room. I don't know how you angels manage to see everyone so quickly. Excellent service nurse, I may see you again soon."

Beaming happily, he limped out of the department and as he left, Marta sidled up to me.

"He comes back, and YOU'RE booking him in." she said.

The fabric chair in which he had originally been sitting had been placed to one side with a sign saying 'do not use' placed across the seat, which was sporting a large, dark stain.

I had a feeling that it was quite likely that he *would* be back and that by seeing him quickly, as opposed to making him wait for over three hours, I had very probably encouraged that. Sometimes, you just can't win.

Why is it that as soon as any of the staff sit down to answer the phone, write notes or fill out a form or two, there's always at least one patient who complains that they've been waiting "ages" to be seen and the nurses and/or doctors are all "sitting around doing nothing"? There is nothing more frustrating than finally finding five minutes to fill in a patient's notes – a legal document by the way – only to have a patient or relative come over to complain that they are "still waiting".

In the waiting room, there is a 'moving message', a board with a moving illuminated message stating the average waiting time at that time, the person in charge of the department that day, and the Emergency Nurse Practitioners on duty. The moving message is changed daily and then updated as and when necessary. It is a very easy thing to change, simply involving using a computer programme on the main office computer. Generally, the person in charge of the department each morning sets the message, but anyone with the correct password can alter it during the day.

One afternoon, I had two sets of notes waiting to be written and whilst waiting for the blood results for one of my patients, I decided to take a few minutes to sit and fill out the notes. Sitting at the desk next to me was Natalie, another staff nurse also with several sets of notes to write.

True to form, within a few minutes of sitting down, a lady approached the desk where I was sitting.

"I'm just wondering how much longer I have to wait," she said, "Only it seems that all of the nurses are having a sit down together and no-one is seeing any of the patients."

Natalie patiently put the woman right and explained that there were several nurses on 'the shop floor' but the reason that they could not be seen working was that they were all busy in cubicles, behind closed curtains, dealing with other people.

Needing to send a district nurse referral form for one of my patients, I went into the main computer to download the necessary form. For some reason, the district nurse site was not playing ball, and after several attempts, I gave up. Whilst I was at the computer, and for no reason other than I was there, I decided to change the moving message on the computer screen. Just for fun, I erased the information on the screen and wrote my own message. Being careful not to hit the 'enter' key, which would have transferred the message to the actual moving message board, and having got various frustrations out of my system, I deleted my message and returned the screen to the original setting.

Going back to the district nurse information, I finally managed to upload the required form, and as I sat trying to fill in all the necessary elements, I heard a commotion coming from the waiting room. Debating whether to go and see what the problem was, I was pre-empted by one of the receptionists putting her head into the office.

"Matron wants to see you, right now," she said.

Knowing that a summons to Matron's office is never good, I set about trying to remember what I had done that might have incurred her wrath this time. I didn't have to wait long. Matron met me in the doorway to her office and, directing me into the waiting room just said "Look at this."

I looked up at where she was pointing and there, lit up in bright red lettering was the moving message proclaiming

"Apologies if you are kept waiting but the doctors and nurses are all very busy sitting on their butts, scoffing Quality Street, discussing Coronation Street and checking their messages on Facebook. We will be with you when we can be bothered."

Oops. Obviously I had not erased my 'message' as I thought and had simply replaced the original proper message with my own sarcastic attempt.

Matron was not impressed and I was 'invited' to attend a Communication Skills refresher course.

≈ 41 ≈

Do You Do Teeth?

Many moons ago, when I first began working in Accident and Emergency, we used to have an emergency dentist working alongside us. He had his own surgery room within the department, brought along his own dental nurse (who was a little bit on the odd side, and I'm sure was probably sharing more than a surgery with him), and they worked most weekends. This was ideal for those patients that did not have a dentist and were complaining of toothache, those patients that had a dentist but their own was shut for the weekend, or for the 'traumatic injuries' caused by little George or Joe having knocked out one of their front teeth playing contact sports.

Unfortunately, for the last twelve years or so, St Josephs has no longer had that service, and dental surgeries *still* close at weekends, on bank holidays and any time before 9am or after five in the afternoon. Consequently, we have many phone calls starting with "I've got pain in my mouth, do you do teeth?"

If these patients do not have their own dentist, a fact becoming more and more common, then they are given the number of an emergency dentist and advised that we can prescribe painkillers and, if necessary, antibiotics, but we do not have dentists in the department and don't "do teeth".

That does not stop the many patients who appear in the department on weekends complaining of toothache and demanding that something be done about their tooth problem. The receptionists will always tell patients that we do not have dentists in the department, but that doesn't stop some patients from asking one of the doctors to "just have a look".

One of our senior registrars saw a patient on Sunday who had been waiting for nearly three hours in the waiting room, with a hand clutched to his face. On examining him, it appeared that this young man had had toothache for six days and he had only come to A/E now because "it doesn't only hurt when I'm sober anymore".

The doctor sympathised with his patient and said that, although he appreciated that the young man *was* in a lot of pain, he could only prescribe pain killers and could not treat the actual source of the pain – the rotting molar in the patient's lower jaw.

"Just put some pliers to it, mate." the patient suggested "I'd do it myself but it hurts."

The doctor explained (for about the fifth time) that he was a doctor and doctors do bodies, not teeth. Dentists do teeth, but we do not have emergency dentists in the Accident and Emergency department any more.

"I can give you tablets to stop it hurting so much." he continued "I can make sure it's not an abscess and I can give you pain killers, but it's still a tooth, and you need a tooth doctor. Tooth doctors are called dentists and they work outside the hospital."

"What? You don't do teeth at all?" he said "I don't need you to fix it, just yank it out."

"If my cat was ill, I would take it to see a cat doctor, in a special veterinary hospital, to get seen and treated," the doctor said. "I would not bring it to A/E to be seen by my colleagues. If I need to have a tooth removed I go to see a dentist. I do not come to A/E to see my colleagues. You need to see a dentist, I shall give you the phone number of an emergency dentist and they should be able to help you."

Pondering this for a minute, the patient said "OK, got that. But could you do it just this once, and then I won't need to come back?" !

≈ 42 ≈

Wrong Number

I spend a lot of time at work. Although only part time, I feel as though I spend more time within the work place than I do at home. This is probably not the case, although I deeply sympathise with those colleagues of mine that work forty plus hours a week, not including those extra days when they have agreed to do an additional shift to cover for a member of staff that has not come in for some reason (the most common being someone calling in sick). Although the Accident and Emergency department, along with other wards and departments, use nurses from the nurse's bank or an agency, it is far more preferable to work with a regular staff member. This does not mean, in any way, shape, or form that bank or agency nurses are inferior or incapable, just that it is always better to work with the devil you know! More than once, I have come on to a shift and been confronted by an agency or bank nurse that has worked in A/E before, although not necessarily in *this* A/E department, and not necessarily in this decade. Consequently, a lot of time and energy is spent in giving a tour of the department, explaining where things are kept, introducing the various members of the team – and then repeating all of this on a regular basis throughout the shift.

I recall having a lovely agency nurse coming to help us one day. She had trained in the 1960s and had just returned to nursing following fifteen years at home to bring up her children. She had recently completed a 'Return to Nursing' course and assured me that she had done quite a lot of Accident and Emergency nursing – although admittedly it was "a while ago". Pleasant and eager to learn she may have been, but it was also a most frustrating day, as in Anne's earlier nursing days patients were fewer and time was less precious. Consequently, she was very popular with the patients that she sat and chatted to for an hour or so whilst gaining a history, but much less so with the regular members of staff who had to keep reminding her that Mr Bloggs or Mrs Jones just happened to be the first of many patients that had to be seen, treated and discharged within a four hour time period. There was also the actual treatments. Despite the Return to Nursing course, there were still minor gaps in Anne's knowledge of emergency treatments, including the fact that we no longer bandage, or splint, broken ribs and soft neck collars are no longer used (research showed that this treatment actually prevented efficient healing in the long run.) This, however, didn't stop Anne from emptying the various cupboards and drawers looking for 'body bandages' and soft collars. By the end of the shift, I felt that Anne had gained a little more knowledge of emergency medicine, and all of the regular staff had worked just that little bit harder than they would had an agency nurse not been employed!

Being at work or home is interchangeable; such is the delight of working shifts. Quite often I have thought to myself "Wow the roads are quiet today," only to realise a little later that it is actually a Sunday, and not Friday or Monday as I had previously thought. It certainly isn't unusual for me to have an entire day at home and only become aware of the day or date when I switch on the six o'clock news on TV that evening.

Answering the telephone, whether at work or home, has caused me some minor problems over the years. Unless I'm expecting a call, the ringing of my home telephone always catches me in the middle of something when I am generally preoccupied. Hence it is no surprise that I have occasionally picked up my home phone and answered "Accident and Emergency Department, Staff Nurse speaking, how may I help you?" This is usually met with either howls of amusement, a stunned silence, or the immediate click as someone thinks that they have dialled an incorrect number and has hung up quickly. My two grown-up daughters are amongst those who not only find this slip up amusing but quite often will invent a 'problem' so that it takes me just that little bit longer to orientate my thoughts and remember that I am, in fact, at home and not answering the department phone at work. However, I am ashamed to say that I never admit this to those people that call back having hung up thinking that they first called a wrong number. If those people happen to mention that they "somehow accidently called the hospital first, before calling the correct number" I make suitably sympathetic noises before murmuring that mistakes of that sort are very easily made!

I am sure that this confusion is quite common amongst people who answer a phone regularly while at work, although uttering my work department and title into the home phone is preferable to making the opposite mistake when answering the telephone situated on the nurses desk.

Only last month I had received several phone calls before leaving the house that morning, all from my son and all asking for me to do various minor tasks for him whilst he was out. I had been at work for just ten minutes when the telephone on the nurses' desk rang and impatiently I snatched it up yelling "What the hell do you want NOW?" into the phone.

Silence. Suddenly I remembered that I was at work and not at home, and someone on the other end of the telephone could be in pain, in distress, or worse.

I quickly began to apologise and whilst doing so the young man butted in saying, "It doesn't matter. I shouldn't have phoned anyway."

Desperately trying to put things right I explained as clearly as I could that I had thought that I was still at home, but only succeeded in sounding as though I was a wee bit simple and a sandwich short of a picnic.

"Really, it's ok," said the young man, "My mum said that it'll work its own way out eventually anyway, and I am sorry to have bothered you."

With that he hung up and, despite my hoping that he would ring back later on in the day, he never did so. I can only hope that whatever it was and wherever it had gone, it had worked its way out without a problem!

Luckily I was the only one near the phone and within earshot on that day. Not so the day that I terminated a call to the path lab with "Ok, thanks very much. Love you, bye."

An audience of several colleagues, a patient or two and the consultant radiologist made sure that I never repeated *that* mistake!

≈ 43 ≈

Language, Timothy!

When in pain, or worried, we are rarely ourselves. Everyone's personality changes when faced with great pain or fear, no matter who we are.

The Catholic church of St Mary's is just down the road from the hospital and has its own convent; a spiritual Order of approximately twelve nuns, most of them quite elderly. On occasion, one of these gentle ladies has had an accident or illness that has necessitated a visit to the Accident and Emergency department and, one Sunday, Sister Mary Bernadette arrived from the convent complaining of a painful right hip. She had tripped over a shallow step on her way to the chapel and landed heavily on her right side. Despite the multiple layers of the habit that she wore, it was still no protection against the hard stone flagged floor that had probably been there for hundreds of years.

Sister Mary Bernadette was quite advanced in years and the general consensus of opinion seemed to be that she had suffered a fracture of the top of the femur, the 'ball' part of the hip joint commonly known as the neck of the femur, which is where the majority of hip fractures occur.

Although she appeared to be in a lot of pain, Sister refused all pain killers other than paracetamol and, as we had yet to help her out of her clothing and into a hospital gown for examination and x-rays, we tried to persuade her to accept something a little stronger.

However, Sister was adamant. Even though it would be painful, she would cope with the pain in her own way.

Fair enough, we certainly did not wish to force medication on the poor lady, and, making sure that she understood that she could have stronger pain killers at any time, we began to help her to remove her many layers of clothing as gently as we could.

Whilst busy with our task, Sister Mary Bernadette apologetically asked if we minded her "using a few rude words" as it would help her to combat the pain.

Secretly delighting in the idea of a nun sitting in a cubicle swearing her head off, we said that if it helped, then to go for it!

Taking a deep breath and clutching her rosary tightly she began chanting:

"Oh flip, flippety flip, flip, flip." Opening her eyes just long enough to apologise for the "rude words" she began again:

"Flipping flip, flipperty flip, flip, flip."

How disappointing: was that *it*? I am afraid to say that I wasn't the only one hoping to hear the odd f-word other than "flip" from the lips of an elderly and very prim and proper nun!

Hearing swear words from a nun is funny, and although it is quite wrong, hearing profanity from a toddler can be even funnier. A child of no more than three years of age came into the department with his dad after falling from his tricycle and hitting his chin. The result was a neat 4cm laceration just on the point of his chin, which was easily treated by a dab of medical glue and a couple of steri-strips. Carefully examining his head and face for any further injuries that might not be visible, I asked Jacob if he had hit his head at all.

"No, only my f***ing face hurts" he said.

Not sure if I had heard him correctly, I repeated the question, saying "Does anything else hurt?"

"Just my f***ing face," he repeated.

Somewhat shocked, I looked towards his dad to gauge his reaction. He sat motionless and didn't say a word.

"So, it's just your chin, then?" I said "We don't need to say the rude f-word do we?"

"It's not rude," said Jacob, "it's what my dad said happened. He said that he was going to have to take me to the hospital now because I've hurt my f***ing face."

It certainly made me think that maybe *I* ought to be a lot more aware of what I say when around small children.

Teenagers using profanity is nothing new. In fact, hearing a teenager in the department effing and blinding is a fairly normal, run of the mill thing. Usually though, they are accompanied by a group of friends and don't have an adult with them.

Limping into the 'Minors' end of the Accident and Emergency Department one day, a pretty blonde girl came in, clutching the arm of her mother for support. They were placed within a cubicle, sat in chairs next to one another and I stood in front of them with my pen poised ready to record the history which led to the girl's injured foot.

At my prompting, twelve year old Kayleigh began to relate the moments leading up to the event.

"You see," she began, "It wasn't even my f***ing fault. My stupid f***ing brother left his soddin' football boots just outside the back door. I stepped out of the door and onto his f***ing boots. My soddin' ankle twisted and I f***ing fell over. Now my f***ing ankle hurts so much I can hardly bloody walk!"

So far, I hadn't written a thing. I looked up and said "How about telling me all of that again, only this time without the swear words?"

Her mother sighed dramatically.

"I'm really sorry, nurse," she said. "I'm always telling her about her language. Every other word that comes out of her f***ing mouth is a bleedin' swear word. I'm f***ing sick of it to tell you the truth!"

≈ 44 ≈

The Mad World of Psychiatry

A good few of our regular patients have well known and well documented psychiatric histories and their attendance in Accident and Emergency is often related to their mental illness. However, there is always room for one or two more and we do see many patients with problems that lead us to believe that a psychiatric evaluation may be well overdue.

A twenty eight year old man walked up to the Accident and Emergency department reception desk and booked himself in with the presenting complaint of "Needing a Liver Transplant". Questioning him further, the receptionist found out that the patient had actually taken an overdose of painkillers the day before and so amended the presenting complaint to "Alleged Overdose" and asked one of the nurses to see the gentleman in the 'Majors' side of the department.

Calling the chap into the department, he was taken into a curtained off bay and asked again why he had attended. Calm as you like, he reiterated that he had attended in order to have a liver transplant.

Insisting on just a *little* more history, it appeared that during yesterday evening, he and his girlfriend had had an argument and after she had walked out on him, slamming the door behind her, he had opened up the medicine cupboard and swallowed the remains of a packet of paracetamol tablets, one caplet at a time, with almost an entire bottle of vodka. He had done this, he said, to "make her sorry".

He stated that he had then "passed out because of all the pills", although the vodka probably had more to do with that than the tablets that he had taken.

Waking up again that morning, he telephoned his friend to tell him about the night before and just happened to mention that he had taken an overdose of paracetamol after his girlfriend had walked out on him. Of course, the way that he told it, it was entirely the fault of his girlfriend that he had taken the medication.

As is always the case, his friend knew someone (probably the ubiquitous friend of a friend) who had once taken a large overdose of paracetamol and had become critically ill with liver failure. The only reason that this particular person was still walking the earth was because he had been lucky enough to have his failing liver replaced by a healthy one donated by a very generous bereaved family.

Anyway, this friend convinced our patient that his liver was now going to shrivel up and die and that the only way that he would survive would be if he had a liver transplant. Hence his visit to Accident and Emergency and his presenting complaint of "Needing a Liver Transplant". He had decided that this was the only way that he would survive the overdose and asked if we could please tell him which ward he was going to be admitted to in order for the procedure to take place. He did realize that there was a waiting list, he said, and so he had brought enough pyjamas for a week or so!

He was most unimpressed when told that he would not be admitted to St Joseph's and would most definitely NOT be having a liver transplant. He was, however, seen by the psychiatric team on duty and admitted to the secure psychiatric unit for evaluation.

Whilst in Accident and Emergency, it was also explained to him that the eight paracetamol tablets that he had deliberately taken the evening before would cause him no harm and in fact, if anything, the bottle of vodka that he had washed the few pills down with had done his liver a lot more harm than the tablets themselves.

Not all patients with a non-physical problem are seen by the psychiatric team. Some obviously abnormal behaviour is deviant as distinct from mental illness and, unsurprisingly, the psychiatric team are not interested in evaluating such patients. This leaves us with no option but to discharge these patients back into the community from whence they came, from where they will no doubt return with a similar 'problem' in a week or so.

One such patient is Brian, who lived in a small rented house just around the corner from the hospital. Brian liked a drink and unfortunately for him his local watering hole was about ten miles away from his home. As he lost his driving licence for drink driving on a regular basis, he had a habit of summoning an ambulance to the pub at the end of his drinking session and giving a history of chest pain, with or without associated shortness of breath. An ambulance would duly be dispatched and arriving at St Joseph's, Brian would immediately discharge himself without being seen and walk the two minutes to his home.

Unfortunately, Brian did have a true history of angina and associated chest pains, and also suffered from breathlessness, probably as a consequence of his years of heavy smoking (he claimed that his chronic obstructive airways disease was due to years of working with "dangerous substances", but as he also claimed to have "been on the dole all my life 'cos there's no jobs going," the true cause of his illness was much more likely to be his 40 a day smoking habit). Consequently, the ambulance service could never be sure whether he really did have a physiological problem requiring hospital treatment, and could not take the risk that he was just after another lift home!

Arriving via ambulance yet again, and again coming from his local hostelry, Brian was seen into the department by Elaine, a newly qualified nurse. Giving a full history of his complaint of chest pain and shortness of breath, he added another problem, hitherto not mentioned to the ambulance crew. Today, he said, he had big problems passing urine and had not managed to go since early that morning. He said that he had a lot of abdominal pain and really needed to pee.

"I'm sure that I just need a catheter in," he explained "last time I couldn't go the nurse put a catheter in and I was right as rain afterwards."

Elaine told him that she would ask the doctor to examine him and if he needed catheterising, then she was sure that someone would do so for him.

"I'd really like you to do it, nurse," he said "It's a really embarrassing thing to have done and I feel comfortable with you."

Elaine muttered something non-committal and went to give one of the doctors her notes and observations on her patient.

The senior house officer examined Brian and established that he did indeed have a full bladder and so noted on his card that part of his treatment would involve the passing of a urinary catheter.

Going back into her patient, Elaine told him that he would be pleased to know that he would be having a catheter inserted and that he should feel more comfortable afterwards. The bad news, she said, was that as a newly qualified nurse, she was not able to perform the procedure but would ask a more experienced colleague to do so for her.

Brian stated that he was disappointed that Elaine could not catheterise him but was sure that the other nurse would be just as gentle "as long as she remembers to warm her hands up!" he quipped.

Twenty minutes later, the curtains were opened and in walked a nurse with a trolley containing a sterilised catheterisation pack and the catheter itself.

"Hi, my name is Henry and I'm here to insert your catheter," he announced as the curtain closed behind him.

"What?" Brian was shocked.

"Your catheter. The one that you told Elaine that you need. I'm here to insert it."

Miraculously, when Brian saw that a man was going to do the procedure, he suddenly recovered his ability to urinate naturally and asked that he be escorted to the toilet as he was sure that he might be able to go without the help of a tube in his bladder!

≈ 45 ≈

And Finally

People are individuals and all people behave in an individual and, sometimes, very unpredictable manner. This is what makes the Human species unique and sets us apart from the rest of the animal kingdom. Some people are 'more evolved' and refined than others in manner, behaviour and in relating to other human beings. But while we have people who insist on damaging themselves and other people, we will always have to have hospitals to treat those people. And within those hospitals will usually be an Accident and Emergency Department of some sort in which to treat the sick and injured. It is deep within the heart of the Accident and Emergency departments right around the country, that you will find the type of hard working and, at times, rather oddly idiosyncratic nurses, doctors and other healthcare staff such as the ones mentioned here.

Although all patients are unique, their stories are all somewhat similar and no matter which hospital that you attend, you will find a Mrs Bamber, a Charlie or a Kayleigh. The names may be different but the people and problems will be much the same. This is what makes these stories so familiar to many people who work in Accident and Emergency departments up and down the country. The names and locations may change but, luckily for those of us employed within the emergency medicine sector, the situations remain pretty well the same. Much as I may moan and complain about the things and people at work, I wouldn't want to be anywhere else. Believe it or not, I do love the work that I do, and the weird and wonderful people that populate my working day. To those patients, I say "thank you" and please keep the weirdness coming for it is what keeps us both sane and amused.

To my long suffering colleagues, what can I say? You know the way it is most days and I deeply admire your patience (no pun intended) and sense of humour. We do more than make a difference to our patients, we also save lives and offer comfort to those that need it. You are all very special people.